THE DOOR HOLDER

THE ART OF LEADERSHIP NAVIGATION: TRANSFORMING CHALLENGES INTO OPPORTUNITIES.

DR.
CIÉ GEE

Copyright ©2025 by Dr. Cie Gee, *The Door Holder: The Art of Leadership Navigation*

Published by Leadership Books, Inc. Las Vegas, NV – New York, NY
LeadershipBooks.com

ISBN Hardcover: 978-1-951648-19-0
eBook: 978-1-951648-23-7
Paperback: 978-1-951648-27-5

All Rights Reserved. No part of this publication may be reproduced, distributed, or transmitted in any form or by any means, including photocopying, recording, or other electronic or mechanical methods without the prior written permission of the publisher, except in the case of brief quotations embodied in critical reviews and certain other noncommercial uses permitted by copyright law.

Leadership Books, Inc. is committed to publishing works of quality and integrity. In that spirit, we are proud to offer this book to our readers; however, the story, the experiences, and the words are the authors alone. The conversations in the book all come from the author's recollections, not word-for-word transcripts. All of the events are true to the best of the author's memory. The author, in no way, represents any company, corporation, or brand mentioned herein. The views expressed are solely those of the author.

Dedication

To all those who held
the Door for me.

CONTENTS

FOREWORD	vii
PREFACE	xi
Introduction: WHY DO YOU HATE ME?	xvii

CHAPTER 1
The Door Holder	1
Show of hands, who thinks they are a Leader?	5
Leadership is an Experience	7
Leadership is Messy	9
Agency (It's not a place).	11

CHAPTER 2
A is for Acknowledgment	19
Pie Crust Promises	19
Wait, you work here? (Lack of Acknowledgment)	21
Yes! You belong here! (Acknowledgment)	26
We have something in common!	28
High School Football	30
The two way one-on-one	33

CHAPTER 3
G is for Growth	39
The Whiny CrossFitter	39
Concrete Bunkers or Fertile Fields	45
Goldilocks Praise	49
Bah Humbug	51
S^2 Specificity and Sincerity	52
Humpty Dumpty Criticism	57
Good Job: You're Fired!	58
Your Praise Sandwich has Expired	59

CHAPTER 4

E is for Empathy — 69
- Ashamed — 69
- Ruled by Rigidity — 73
- Empathetic Respect — 76
- The Forgotten Beans — 77
- No, You're a MOM — 82
- Hitchhikers — 85

CHAPTER 5

N is for Needs — 91
- A Badge of Burnout — 91
- Inconvenient Sick Leave — 94
- Psychological Safety — 98
- Everything is Fine! Ignore the Fire — 102
- I don't know, and that's okay — 106

CHAPTER 6

C is for Confidence — 111
- Salad Fork — 111
- Muzzle the Noise — 114
- Obedience Training — 120
- Confidence Vampires — 124
- A Tale of Two Leaders — 126
- Confidence to Trust — 134
- A Pompous Circumstance — 134

CHAPTER 7

Y is for You — 143
- Oxygen Mask — 144
- Fun with Failure — 146
- Memory Lane — 147
- Emotional Intelligence — 157
- K2 — 162

FOREWORD

I've always had a love for leadership, and I've been blessed to train on leadership, be an executive coach, and a leader myself. So, when Cié told me she was writing a book about leadership inspired by a personal moment that pushed her boundaries, I was intrigued. Knowing Cié as a leader, I couldn't even wonder what could push her boundaries in the first place. What was this situation or story that encouraged her to write such a book?

Every day, I encounter acts of leadership all around me. And, it's not always from the head "honcho in charge." I see individuals leading by example, setting vision, motivating and inspiring people. What I never paused to really reflect upon was the simple question, "What do they have in common?" After reading the book, that a-ha moment was laid bare—they hold the door for others. Cié's book shows how leadership translates into action. It shows how with small acts of kindness, courage, and selflessness, the leaders of tomorrow can be developed and formed by the leaders of today.

Reading the book reminded me of a story about Cié. About 15 years ago, she and I served together on a regional board of directors. We were assigned to travel to a state organization's meeting to give a report, do some conference sessions, and represent the regional organization to the state membership. As we headed back home from Arkansas, we stopped for lunch in a small diner, and at that lunch table, Cié opened up to me about a variety of topics that were on her mind. I listened, and then did what comes naturally to me—I encouraged her and helped her find her own answers by asking questions. What I didn't realize was that in that moment, I held the door for Cié in a way that she has since said was very meaningful and empowering to her. Little did either of us know that in that moment, she would write a book about holding the door for others.

The Door Holder is a concise and engaging read that will answer, as the author states in the title, how to transform challenges into opportunities. What I find limiting about most leadership books is they are chock full of little pearls of wisdom, but rarely provide an actionable plan for implementation, or opportunities for workbook style pauses. Leadership is a blend of art and science, so we must have more than theory to accomplish leadership in the real world. Cié does a fabulous job of bridging this gap for the reader in a way that makes one reflect, take note, and process through one's own style. And, she makes it possible for us to realize that as leaders, the relationships we forge with others is an act of selfless service.

The Door Holder provides more than a roadmap. Through a variety of true-life vignettes that make it easy for the reader to imagine oneself in the same situation, we walk away with formative responses to leadership that lead to outcomes and action—not summative checklists. If anything, the reader understands the art of leadership as transformational, not transactional.

As you read the book, it will become evident that Cié walks the talk because her results are mingled with stories around the results of herself AND others. I have been privileged to witness Cié on her leadership journey for almost 20 years, now. She has had ups and downs, moments of doubt, flashes of inspiration, and opportunities that have stretched her out of her comfort zone. What I have observed through all of this is that she did two things: she looked at every instance as a possibility to learn and grow, and she paused in each moment to understand that what she learned needed to be parlayed into opportunities for others. I admire Cié – simply by writing this book, she has once again held the door by sharing her voice and her journey so that others can learn, act, implement, and engage as effective leaders in their own leadership journey.

As Malcolm Gladwell points out in his book *The Outliers*, the key to achieving true expertise in any skill is simply a matter of practicing, albeit in the correct way, for at least 10,000 hours. Cié has translated her 10,000 hours into this digestible and easy to comprehend book that focuses on leadership as a somewhat messy experience that leads to developing self and others in meaningful ways. We walk away understanding that leadership is about agency. Her gift is the art of illumination through story-telling, leaving you as the reader, with someone at the other end of the door waiting with an unrestricted pathway to simply walk through.

The examples and lessons Cié portrays in the book come from years of her own personal leadership lab—trials and triumphs, lessons learned by making mistakes, and moments of leaning in when in doubt. But, most importantly, they transpire from moments of authenticity, vulnerability, and genuineness about putting others first and simply holding the door as an act of kindness, learning, and empowerment. The strategies she provides will surely help you uncover blind spots so that you can elevate your own leadership to improve overall team performance, create a culture of employee engagement, and develop the type of leaders we all want to see for our future.

Dr. Jacquelyn D. Elliott
President Emerita, enrollmentFUEL
CXO, Blue Rock Search

PREFACE

It was 6:00 a.m. A Friday, in September. The text message came through simultaneously with my wake-up alarm. In a groggy state I struggled to multitask reading the message and silencing the alarm in tandem. The text message was from the guest speaker, Dr. Sterling, the person we had coordinated to lead the entire first day of a yearlong leadership development program. A *leadership development program* that was for developing executive leadership, which meant all the participants were already leaders in their field. A *leadership development program* that I had recently been asked to take over. A *leadership development program* that this very guest speaker had founded and led for five years before me. Since Dr. Sterling was such a pivotal reason the program even existed, she was invited to be the opening facilitator to help set the tone and transition. She was a fantastic presenter, facilitator, and leader.

Dr. Sterling was the former Vice President, having moved on to another company. The day she announced she was leaving, I received a companywide email announcing her departure, then almost immediately a personal email request asking me to meet with her one-on-one. It was at this meeting that she asked, *no told,* me that I was the one she had chosen to take over the leadership program. My self-doubt tried to protest but Dr. Sterling wouldn't allow it.

At her going away party she gave me a hug. In a scene reminiscent of a dramatic movie, she squeezed a little tighter and whispered, "keep the program going, don't let it fail."

So, yeah, no pressure at all.

Once my eyes focused, I read the text.

> Hi Cié, I'm sorry, but I am sick and cannot lead the program today.

My heart began to pound as my mind raced at how to handle this situation. She was leading the *whole* day. She was chosen because of her ability to set the climate for the *whole* year. In retrospect I believe I invited her for the first day so I could baby step into this new role. She was a metaphorical security blanket so I would not be thrown into the deep end of leading a group of leaders. I was too afraid of drowning. *Cancel, I will just cancel the event.* Then another text came.

> You need to lead it. I know you can. You know the material. You will be amazing!

I *had* worked with the program for a few years; I did *know* the material. *I just had to decide if I could do it.* Stumbling around in my mind I came up with a million catastrophizing events. What if people objected because I'm not Dr. Sterling? What if they got bored? What if they ask questions I could not answer? What if I fail?

But… what if I succeed?

Getting dressed quickly, I rushed to work to prepare and inform my fellow facilitators that we were running the show and I would lead the activities that Dr. Sterling was supposed to lead. As the new cohort of the program started arriving, I smiled and welcomed them trying to create the environment of belonging that Dr. Sterling always cultivated. I led the activities; I led the day's programming with all my heart and soul. At the closing of the day, I collected all the paper evaluations from participants on how the day went and shoved them in my purse. As it started to rain, I sprinted to my car to have a safe place to look at them in private. I was preparing myself for any negative feedback that might leap off the pages and attack me. Damp from the rain, and with a lump in my throat, I read the first evaluation, the second, tenth, twentieth. No attack came. The feedback was all positive comments, and a reoccuring theme of enthusiasm for the next session. The only negative comment was about the lack of ginger ale among the soda selection which made me snort with relieved laughter! I texted Dr. Sterling.

> The day went perfectly, thank you for trusting and believing in me.

At 6:00 a.m. that Friday morning in September I had to do *something*. I had to make a choice. Why did I choose to act instead of cancel? How did I proceed without my 'security blanket' in a leadership situation?

As I progressed along in my own leadership journey I was constantly asking myself this question. What contributes to that sense of action, that belief that one can step into ambiguity or uncomfortableness and act? When the outcome is unknown, what fuels the determination to move forward and deal with whatever result may arise?

With a healthy background in interpersonal communication, I am conditioned to observe and analyze how our interactions with others create certain results. In leading people and being led by others I became fascinated with what made healthy, productive teams, and what environments created unhealthy, inefficient, low morale teams. What leaders made me want to push my boundaries and what leaders made me just want to quit.

This book was largely inspired by the events of 2020. Not only the pandemic, but the political and societal events that made that year unprecedented. I had assumed a new executive leadership role of a large unit in summer of 2019. This meant I had only been with them less than a year when we were all sent home and were suddenly faced with events none of us had ever experienced. Suddenly so much more was required of me as a leader. I found myself in a forced time of reflection that brought me back to that original question: what made healthy teams, and what environments created unhealthy teams? This book is a product of several years of questioning, researching, and self-reflecting in finding an answer to that question.

I have credentials, two degrees in interpersonal communication and one in leadership. I've published and spoken on this topic for years, but what really made me want to write this book was the ugly, messy, sometimes incredibly frustrating journey that is leadership. I don't feel like we talk about that enough. Sometimes we talk about the glory of leadership but fail to talk about the fact that it scares people, it's plagued with self-doubt, and sometimes we as leaders just fail.

This book illustrates proven ways to improve your relationship with leadership and create amazing, effective, and motivated teams. It is written vulnerably authentic, and therefore you have permission to be authentic too. My hope is that it provides practical tools that you can start using immediately to create that healthy and productive professional environment. Learn to cultivate a team that will act and not cancel. Learn to be the leader you were meant to be.

I'm holding the door for you, please join me.

Introduction

WHY DO YOU HATE ME?

"Cié, Why do you hate me?" Claudia asked with a worried yet determined look on her face.

Claudia was my direct report. I had only been supervising her for about four months and she thought I hated her. *So, this was how my leadership journey was going.*

Out of nowhere, I was slammed with this question, as we were coming back from a meeting. We both stopped walking and just stared at each other. I, with a confused look and her a stern gaze on the verge of tears. Understanding the public space we found ourselves in was not the place to have this unpleasant exchange, I suggested we return to my office and discuss the roots behind this inquiry.

Claudia was working in the entry-level position I started my career in years before. After five years, I was promoted to lead that office. In my mind, I was doing all the things a Leader was supposed to do. I checked all the boxes, attending workshops, reading books, and watching Ted Talks. I participated in the essential Leadership development program and presented at various conferences. I was doing everything right and Claudia was obviously incorrect in her assumptions.

How could she possibly think I hated her?

We uncomfortably walked back to my office for the conversation neither of us was looking forward to. The tension was palpable as I closed the Door and took a deep breath. After two hours, where tears were shed, and difficult things were revealed, we reached a point of understanding and a path forward. And I reached a point of humble Leadership awareness. Claudia's question was **not** out of nowhere. It was warranted.

Reflecting on how I was leading, I understood how the perception of dislike was formed. It was a culmination of tiny events that built up over time. I hadn't realized what it had become.

I came into supervision after she was hired, so I never onboarded her or discussed expectations. In my mind, I didn't want to disrupt the flow.

I never dropped by to say *good morning* because I had a past supervisor that would walk the office at 8:00 am to check on who had arrived on time and who had not. I didn't want it to seem like I was monitoring her arrival.

I never attempted to get to know her beyond her title and job description, never asking about her desire for growth or passions. I didn't want to pry.

I assigned tasks through email with very little explanation or offer of support. Claudia was smart, and I didn't want it to seem like I was questioning her ability. I didn't want to insult her intelligence.

In an attempt to avoid micromanaging, I simply *ignored* her. I offered no praise or criticism. I took the approach of *'good Leaders just get out of the way'* too literally.

But my rationalizations for my actions were just excuses. As a new Leader, I had a lot of insecurities about my ability to lead effectively. I was following an imaginary script that dictated what Leaders should and should not do. In retrospect, I felt the tensions between Claudia and me and the lag in productivity, but my desire to pretend everything was fine kept me silent. My actions had this talented young professional ready to quit. I needed to make a change in how I perceived Leadership. And it took getting real with humility, vulnerability, and answering the questions of why. Why do I want to lead?

Leadership development in the form of programming, books, and talks is everywhere, but is it working? How many books have you read, or workshops have you attended to improve Leadership or improve your team? Do you find yourself in these situations:

- You still aren't seeing results either in yourself or in your team.
- You lack confidence as a Leader or have certain fears about leading.
- You have unmotivated employees or a high turnover rate.
- There is no viable candidate on your team to be promoted to a Leadership position.
- You struggle with uncomfortable professional conversations and difficult personalities.

If you said yes to any of these, keep reading.

Leadership cannot happen inside your own head. For Leadership to work, you must forge a relationship with those you lead and ensure they are on the journey with you.

The following pages are full of every practical, inspirational, messy, fall down, and get back up Leadership lesson I have learned from WHY DO YOU HATE ME until now. To benefit from the ideas in this book, you, as the reader, must let go of past assumptions and re-evaluate your good intentions. Approach the stories in this book with curiosity and humility. Open yourself up to see things from a different perspective. I promise it works.

> **LEADERSHIP CANNOT HAPPEN INSIDE YOUR OWN HEAD.**

Before we get into the good stuff...

What happened to Claudia? Claudia is now Dr. Claudia. She rose to lead that office and beyond. Years later, we turned that pivotal interaction into a conference presentation. And we still seek each other out for Leadership advice. From that day forward, our relationship changed, and I became more intentional with my Leadership approaches. Was I perfect after that? No, not at all, nor am I perfect now, but altering my mindset about Leadership, especially about my own self-concept, and actually putting in the work that all the books and workshops talk about resulted in growth in myself and those I lead more than I ever could have imagined.

I was trying to be the Line Leader when I needed to be a Door Holder. Come with me on a Leadership journey and discover how to ignite passion in not only yourself but also your teams and achieve the results you are looking for. Turn those challenges you are facing into opportunities.

I'm holding the Door for you, but what does it mean to be a Door Holder?

Chapter 1

THE DOOR HOLDER

It was your typical rural Texas farming community in the late 1980s. The obligatory Dairy Queen and Friday night football games. More dirt roads than paved. More pick-up trucks than cars. Being rural, it would only have the three required schools: elementary, middle, and high school. This is where I grew up and learned Leadership's true meaning. It just took many years to figure it out.

Overall, I was a good kid in elementary school. The main scolding I received was for being a tattletale and for talking. Spelling wasn't my strong suit (and still isn't), and I was not athletic. In second grade, I declared that I wanted to be a paleontologist (and still do).

In fourth and fifth grade, one of the highlights of coming into the classroom each morning was looking to the right of the Door to see who the Line Leader would be for the day. The Line Leader was the chosen student who led the class to and from all the critical activities. To see MY name in perfect cursive on a laminated rectangle stuck by the Door was euphoric. I was labeled by someone in authority as **the Leader.**

There were four critical duties the Line Leader had to perform:

1. Lead the line to recess.
2. Lead the line to lunch.
3. Lead the line to gym.
4. Lead the line to outside pick up after school.

The glory of being the Line Leader came from the fact that the Line Leader was the first to all these highly sought-after destinations. The first one to burst out on the playground and claim one of the coveted spots on top of the monkey bars. The first one to lunch, where you got to sit down first and start eating, so there was more time for talking (and if it was taco boat day, a chance at second helpings). The first one to gym to claim a firm basketball instead of a half-flat one that wouldn't dribble. And the first one out after school was over.

Leading the line was fun.
Leading the line was easy.
Leading the line had perks.

But the euphoria did not last. The next day, your name was still to the right of the Door, but you had a different job. The Door Holder. Someone else's name was in the Line Leader spot, and your name was moved down. The Door Holder's job was to start walking behind the Line Leader, hold the Door for the entire class and bring up the end of the line.

I hated being the Door Holder.

We all knew the job of Door Holder ranked last, even after chalkboard distributor and paper collector. It was not popular because it was not easy; it was hard work and came with sacrifices.

When I was the Door Holder, I never got a spot on the monkey bars because I was last to recess.

At lunch, I had to sit at the spillover table. Humiliating. And you can forget about a double helping on taco boat day. Lunch, as it turns out, was a trifecta of misery for the Door Holder. On the way to lunch, there were two Doors; you had to hold the Door, then run back up to the front of the line just to hold the Door again and still be last.

Gym class was a basket of disappointment as well. I was not athletic to begin with, and by being last, I always got the flat basketball.

Even the final Door Holding of the day was tainted. As I held the Door for the students to leave school, other classes would take advantage and run through, making me get outside for pick up even later.

The Door Holder also had added responsibility. The Door Holder's obligation was to decide when the line could pass through the Door. If there was another class in the way, the Door Holder had to decide to try and shove everyone through quickly or wait to let the line pass. Inevitably, someone would stop to tie their shoe, randomly fall down, or stare off into space and forget to move. The Line Leader was easy; they just walked to the destination, never worrying about what was happening behind them.

If it was raining, the Door Holder always got wetter.

When it was hot, the Door Holder always got sweatier.

I hated being the Door Holder.

When I started my professional career, I would look for the Line Leaders, the ones out in front, who were arriving first, speaking first, and blazing ahead. When I defined the term Leader in my head, I pictured and aspired to be this. I put Leadership on a pedestal. I wrote it in cursive on a laminated square to the right of the Door.

With Claudia I tried the Line Leader mentality. I was the one marching in front, I didn't need to stay back and hold the Door for her. I assumed she would just be happy to follow along. I struggled with trying to achieve that Line Leader euphoria. I might reach the destination, but that didn't matter if no one reached it with me.

You aren't a Line Leader without a line. You are just wandering around.

I've seen many Line Leaders who morph into Door Slammers or Door Lockers because they have zero concern for the line they are leading, or like me, believe their laminated square philosophy is working. I was a Door Slammer and didn't even realize it.

But just as it was in that elementary school hallway, the Door Holders kept the line from falling into chaos. It's the patient hand, looking ahead as well as behind. It's the awareness of everyone in the line, where they are, who they are, and how you can help them get to the destination. Understanding your faults and what you can learn from each member as they pass through the Door.

Miraculous changes began to occur when I started leading as the Door Holder.

Think about the people that made an impact on your professional life. The ones that coached you, taught you, challenged you. The ones that didn't ignore you. Was it the Line Leader that marched ahead, never looking back, never checking on your progress? Or was it the Door Holder, who stopped and held the Door for you, waited for you, and helped you when you fell? Was it someone that supported YOU so that YOU could reach the destination and not be left behind?

I would not be where I am today (professionally or personally) if it wasn't for all the amazing Door Holders along the way. The funny thing about Door Holders is that we sometimes don't even realize they held the Door for us until we are miles on the other side.

This book is not only for Leaders to understand how to make better teams, but also a self-study on Leadership. Are you a Line Leader or a Door Holder? Are you leading your team, never looking back, or are you holding the Door, making sure everyone is getting to the destination?

SHOW OF HANDS, WHO THINKS THEY ARE A LEADER?

Every time I give a presentation or a workshop on Leadership, I start with the same question, *who thinks they are a Leader?*

Every time about 1/3 or less of the room raises their hand, the rest look around to see if they *should* raise their hand. It's like I've asked a complicated math problem, and people are trying to calculate the correct answer to know if a + b = Leader.

Defining a Leader is tricky. Some people justify their Leadership label because they have the right spot on the organizational chart. "I have a title that makes people report to me, so I guess I'm a Leader."

Others say, "I do their performance evaluations and approve the paychecks, so that makes them follow me."

Just because someone reports to you, doesn't necessarily make you a Leader.

Why is it so difficult to enthusiastically claim the role of a Leader? Because it's not always a one size fits all.

> **JUST BECAUSE SOMEONE REPORTS TO YOU, DOESN'T NECESSARILY MAKE YOU A LEADER.**

Leadership is often discussed in styles or types. We are asked to identify with what type we are: servant, visionary, autocratic, narcissistic, constructivist, strategic, and the list goes on. This can feel absolute. Each of these styles has different definitions. For example, servant Leadership is described as having a deep sense of caring for those you lead.[1] Visionary is practical and inspirational, and knows where to go, how to get there, and can motivate others.[2]

---

1. Greenleaf, Robert K. *Servant Leadership: A Journey into the Nature of Legitimate Power and Greatness*. Mahwah, NJ: Paulist Press, 2002.
2. Graham, Jill W. "Servant-Leadership in Organizations: Inspirational and Moral." *The Leadership Quarterly* 2, no. 2 (1991): 105-119.

Narcissistic is overconfidence, extraversion, dominance, high self-esteem, and superficial charm.[3]

Sometimes people get stuck on these labels or believe that merely by stating, "I'm a servant Leader," they are doing their best.

Leadership is situational, nuanced, and complex.

Let's agree that Leadership can be difficult to define.

LEADERSHIP IS AN EXPERIENCE

Leadership isn't a static thing, a label, or a word. It's action, it's interpersonal, it's fluid, it's an experience. Leadership is a relationship.[4] There is nothing more fluid than a relationship. The professional space is an interpersonal sphere of influence where we persuade people to spend time and energy on something: to motivate, to get people to act for the right reason, care about the work, the collaboration, and the organization. We have to go beyond the transactional.

People act the way they do for a reason. That's why Leadership holds such a higher responsibility than managers. As a manager, I can tell you how to do it, what to do, and when to do it. But that's not holding the Door. Many Leaders are just managers in disguise.

Leadership does not happen in a vacuum but is influenced by the context in which it operates.[5] We need to recognize

---

3. Nevicka, Barbara, Annebel De Hoogh, Annelies Van Vianen, Bianca Beersma, and Doris McIlwain. "All I Need Is a Stage to Shine: Narcissists' Leader Emergence and Performance." *The Leadership Quarterly* 22, no. 5 (2011): 910-925.
4. Kouzes, James M., and Barry Z. Posner. *The Leadership Challenge*. San Francisco: Jossey-Bass, 2007.
5. Sun, Peter Y. T. "The Servant Identity: Influences on the Cognition and Behavior of Servant Leaders." *The Leadership Quarterly* 24, no. 4 (2013): 544-557.

that Leadership today operates in a different context than in years past. Many places of work operate in crisis mode more often now than ever. These are periods of uncertainty, disruption, and change which require Leaders to take actions that bring about immediate change in behavior, beliefs, and outcomes.[6] This requires a more adaptive behavior on the part of the Leader and on the part of the follower. But allowing space for that adaptive behavior is critical. This means Leaders need to be more person-focused, able to collaborate with others and create shared direction, alignment, and commitment between social groups that span different generations and perspectives.

> **LEADERSHIP IS A RELATIONSHIP BUILT THROUGH EXPERIENCE**

It is no longer enough to passively operate as a Leader. It is also no longer applicable to say that those who are 'good' Leaders are just more courageous than ordinary people.[7] Also, moving forward isn't about the skill or talent of the Leader. Individuals and groups must work collaboratively in order to achieve outcomes. It has become necessary to maximize the contributions many more individuals can make.[8] This requires an understanding of why people think and behave in certain ways, which can lead to better engagement no matter

---

6. Bundy, Jonathan, and Michael D. Pfarrer. "A Burden of Responsibility: The Role of Social Approval at the Onset of a Crisis." *Academy of Management Review* 40, no. 3 (2015): 345-369.
7. Shah, Jessica. "Three Psychological Traits Effective Leaders Know How to Manage." *Fast Company*, October 13, 2015. Accessed in 2020. https://www.fastcompany.com/3052136/3-psychological-traits-effective-leaders-know-how-to-manage.
8. Bolden, Richard, Aman Gulati, and Gareth Edwards. "Mobilizing Change in Public Services: Insights from a Systems Leadership Development Intervention." *International Journal of Public Administration* 43, no. 1 (2020): 26-36.

what challenges are faced.[9] This means appreciating a person for who they are, even if their opinions differ from yours or if they don't handle situations like you do.

As in the elementary school example, no one was always the Line Leader or the Door Holder. It's the experience of navigating through Leadership situations (trial and error) as well as following and leading that builds someone into a Leader. We learn from leading the line, holding the door, and from just being in the line. It is a longitudinal learning process.[10]

Let's agree that Leadership is a relationship built through experience.

LEADERSHIP IS MESSY

When I facilitated a Leadership development course, a common request (and complaint) was the need for a *set-it-and-forget-it* Leadership guide. A checklist or cheat sheet for all Leadership conundrums. People wanted a *script* for difficult conversations and a step-by-step playbook for instant effective teams. It's not that straightforward.

Before my professional career, I was an actress in a local theater. I was paid for my participation which qualifies me to claim the 'actress' title, even though it barely covered the gas to drive to the theater. Rehearsals would last for one month, and the show would run every Friday, Saturday, and Sunday for a month and a half. We all had the same script, but no two shows were ever the same.

---

9. Shah, "Three Psychological Traits"
10. O'Connell, Patrick K. "A Simplified Framework for 21st Century Leader Development." *The Leadership Quarterly* 25, no. 2 (2014): 183-203.

Small changes such as an actor feeling ill, someone being late for their scene, or even an argument between actors off stage could change the flow of the play. Yes, people forgot their lines or accidentally said someone else's line but as a team, we were prepared for these unexpected occurrences.

We had all practiced improvisation, or the art of spontaneity, making something out of what you have to keep things moving in a desired direction. Improvisation is messy; sometimes it works beautifully, and sometimes it is clunky and rough. But we couldn't just stop and ask for the script. We had to keep going. We had all learned through experience how to make the scene work, even when it was off script.

In Leadership, you can't stop and ask for the script. There is no script. I argue no one had a *'Leadership during a Pandemic'* script back in 2020. We must accept that not knowing is okay. Improvisation is not knowing what comes next; you are simply using the cues from your environment to create. The confidence to be flexible as a Leader and appreciate the many different options your team brings to the table is critical. The courage to experiment comes from the experience. And sometimes experiments are messy. You have permission to allow for a mess as you travel through this book.

Let's agree that Leadership is messy.

Taking what we agree:

1. Leadership is hard to define,
2. Leadership is a relationship through experience,
3. Leadership is messy.

There isn't a leadership template that applies to every situation. You have to create the Leadership that is needed in your particular space with those who are in your charge. This takes the ability to be dynamic, adaptive, and forward-thinking. And to build the capacity for those you lead to walk confidently through the Door, those you lead must possess these abilities too. How do we do this?

The answer is we must develop Agency within ourselves and others.

AGENCY (IT'S NOT A PLACE).

Agency is the faith and belief in ourselves to move rather than being static or stationary. It is the ability to act autonomously and freely. It refers to people who feel they can coordinate learning skills, motivation, and emotions to reach desired goals.[11]

If you have a strong sense of Agency, you can control challenging environmental demands by taking adaptive action. Adaptive action is a mindset that allows us to navigate uncertainties, be nimble during times of change, and make intentional choices in dynamic environments.

Agency is not about having it all figured out. It's the belief that you *can* figure it out or, rather, figure something out and move forward. It's the belief that you can make a change and deal with whatever outcomes may arise.[12]

How many times do we pause on taking adaptive action? We are in some cognitive distress, but we do not say anything for fear of something we have created in our heads. Fear of

---
11. Bandura, Albert. "Exercise of Human Agency through Collective Efficacy." *Psychological Science* 9, no. 3 (2000): 75-78.
12. Bandura, "Exercise of Human Agency"

failure, ridicule, disappointment, or even just fear of making a decision. Maybe it isn't fear; it's apathy. We have checked out, so we are running out the clock.

Who do you want to be? Who do you want on your team? Agents of change or apathetic clock watchers?

Individuals are producers of experiences.

We need to believe that we can produce desired effects by our actions so we have more incentive to act.[13] Current conditions require Leaders to intentionally meet the professional context's complex challenges, therefore, it is critical to have Agency to positively influence teams and the organization's culture, climate, and performance.[14]

To mobilize groups toward collective performance, Leaders have to exercise high levels of personal Agency and create similar levels of Agency in those individuals they lead by proxy.[15]

> **YOU AREN'T AS APPREHENSIVE IF YOU BELIEVE YOU CAN EXERCISE CONTROL OVER POTENTIAL THREATS.**

Leaders sometimes get micro-focused on tasks and projects instead of the people they are leading. People do not operate in a vacuum, therefore, attention to the professional climate is a must.[16] There will be difficulties, there will be unexpected events that cause quick decisions, and there will be times of stress. Suppose the general mode of the team is to think in self-enhancing ways instead of self-debilitating ways,

---

13. Bandura, "Exercise of Human Agency"
14. Hannah, Sean T., Bruce J. Avolio, Fred Luthans, and Peter D. Harms. "Leadership Efficacy: Review and Future Directions." *The Leadership Quarterly* 19, no. 6 (2008): 669-692.
15. Bandura, "Exercise of Human Agency"
16. Hannah, "Leadership Efficacy"

the motivation to persevere in the face of difficulties. In that case, their well-being will be greater, and their vulnerability to stress will be less.[17] This means the difference between someone who thinks erratically versus strategically and optimistically versus pessimistically.[18] A high sense of Agency allows people to choose to perform more challenging tasks, set higher goals, and recover faster from setbacks.

You aren't as apprehensive if you believe you can exercise control over potential threats. However, if you think you cannot manage potential threats, you will experience anxiety.

Agency isn't a label you can suddenly give someone, just like a title doesn't automatically make you a Leader. Building Agency doesn't require any special training or advanced degree. You can't have Amazon deliver it or take a supplement. In writing this book, I was trying to figure out how my Agency strengthened into what it is today. That's when I started thinking about my Leadership journey and all the Door Holders along the way. It's a messy process with many twists and turns. We will explore different ways to build Agency within yourself and others to have the ability to hold the Door.

Having more Agency means acknowledging the power of your situation. We will never improve if we don't believe that we are in control of our improvement. We place limitations on ourselves consciously and unconsciously. Why? We are influenced by what we are exposed to and naturally develop misconceptions about what it means to be a Leader. When we accept that we are not perfect shiny Leaders but messy,

---

17. Bandura, Albert, and Edwin A. Locke. "Negative Self-Efficacy and Goal Effects Revisited." *Journal of Applied Psychology* 88, no. 1 (2003): 87-99.
18. Bandura, "Exercise of Human Agency"

lifelong learning Leaders, we open ourselves up with the freedom to develop other Leaders. This takes vulnerability and a dash of humility.

The Door Holder is a Leadership journey incorporating varying Leadership styles depending on the situation. I believe there isn't one Leadership style that is always applicable. Sometimes servant Leadership style is best, while other times, an authoritative approach is needed. And in rare, specialized circumstances, narcissistic Leadership applies.

Approaching Leadership situations with the Door Holder mentality means focusing on the desire to grow and improve yourself and those you lead. It's about growing Agency.

Here are some real-world examples of Agency:

- The belief that you can make a change from right where you are now is Agency.
- Deciding to leave a toxic job for mental and physical health is Agency.
- Seeing potential in an employee and reorganizing or reassigning work tasks so they can excel and grow is Agency.
- Growing up in an adverse environment and making the decision that your future will be different and taking the steps to change it is Agency.
- Speaking up against unethical/discriminatory situations is Agency.
- Inheriting a group of low morale employees and deciding to motivate and inspire them is Agency.
- Having the confidence to own a project even though you don't have all the answers is Agency.

- Questioning the legitimacy and relevance of an antiquated rule is Agency.
- Stopping the status quo that is not working and making your own path is Agency.
- Advocating for a salary increase to match your worth or doing this for another in your charge is Agency.
- Telling your internal negative self-talk to *shut up* is Agency.
- Asking 'why' is Agency.
- Saying 'no' to something when you are overloaded or burned out is Agency.
- Understanding that 'no' is a complete sentence is Agency.
- Taking a vacation and not checking emails so you can recharge is Agency.
- Realizing that you have the power to be an authentic Leader is Agency.
- Holding the Door for others is Agency.

You have the power to open new Doors and hold them open to new pathways. In the following chapters I'll make a case for why being the Door Holder is a powerful Leadership philosophy because it involves exerting your own Agency WHILE, at the same time, enabling you to increase Agency in others. This is a book about lifting others up, because when we lift others, we rise as well.

We will go back to the elementary way of organizing and remembering to tackle this discovery of Agency one letter at a time.

A is for Acknowledgment

We will discover simple yet effective ways to make people feel a sense of belonging.

G is for Growth

We will explore ways to help people develop professionally.

E is for Empathy

We will discuss the importance of understanding where someone is coming from.

N is for Needs

We will delve into what makes a healthy, psychologically safe environment.

C is for Confidence

We will investigate building confidence within yourself and your team.

Y is for You

We will focus on leading yourself with compassion and care.

WHO AM I?

As the author of this book, you will get to know me quite well. All the stories are from my leadership journey either with me in the lead role, as a supporting character, or sometimes watching from the audience. But until we get there…

- I'm the kid who held the Door for you in fourth grade.
- I'm the new Leader who doubted themselves.
- I'm someone who embraces failing forward and learning every day.
- I'm not a Leadership superhero. I'm just Cié from rural Texas. Authenticity is better than an imaginary cape.
- I'm a Door Holder, or at least I try every day to be one for real people who do real amazing work. Real people were Door Holders for me.
- I'm holding the Door for you. Let's go!

"If you want to build a ship don't drum up people to collect wood and don't assign them tasks and work, but rather teach them to long for the endless immensity of the sea."

— *Antoine de Saint-Exupéry*

Chapter 2

A IS FOR ACKNOWLEDGMENT

Acknowledgment: Acceptance of the truth or existence of something/someone.

PIE CRUST PROMISES

As my grandmother used to say (and also Mary Poppins), that's a pie crust promise easily made, easily broken.

Monica was a mid-level professional who just received a promotion through an organizational restructure. Her work ethic and ability to deliver propelled her to the promotion.

Olivia, her new supervisor, was also a female who had achieved great strides in a male-dominated field. Monica was eager to work with Olivia.

In the beginning, Olivia expressed excitement about collaborating with Monica, and Olivia would say things like, "I get ideas driving to work, so I can't wait to chat with you over coffee and brainstorm" or "I'm looking forward to your skills and talents improving the organization."

Monica was over the moon with excitement.

Since the reorganization was fast, there were unanswered questions about her new role, so she mapped out action items for the top-priority projects to make meetings as productive as possible with Olivia.

Monica started her new role, but the coffee chats never came. Monica would arrive early to be ready for those *driving to work ideas*, but the brainstorms never occured. Olivia was rarely even in the office, and when she was, her Door usually was closed. Monica attempted to move forward with ideas and projects, but Olivia would tell her to wait before moving forward so they could discuss. Then she would either cancel their meetings without rescheduling or simply not show up. To make matters worse, Monica's office was in the same office suite as Olivia's, and in the eight months she worked in that position, Olivia only came into Monica's office twice. Olivia didn't welcome her on board, coach her, or acknowledge her. She said all the right things in the beginning, but they became pie crust promises, easily made, easily broken. Monica's excitement deteriorated; the passion crumbled.

Would it surprise you to know that one of the main reasons for someone leaving a position or feeling a work environment is negative is because they feel ignored or undervalued.[19] In this case Monica left before the year was up. The words and actions of a Leader are immensely powerful and should be used with great caution. I've heard from many exceptional employees who have left a position because of pie-crust promises or a general lack of acknowledgment from their Leader. In fact, I am one of them who chose to leave.

The simple act of acknowledgment, whether acknowledging the efforts, ideas, and contributions or simply acknowledging that someone works in your area, is a huge factor in employee morale and is critical in being a Door Holder. In the next few pages, we will explore the act of acknowledgment from the very basic to the more in-depth. These ideas are easily implemented; it just takes a little time and acknowledgment that a change in approach is needed.

WAIT, YOU WORK HERE? (LACK OF ACKNOWLEDGMENT)

How do these statements make you feel? Do you believe these individuals felt acknowledged?

"I've worked here for three weeks and still haven't met my boss."

"Our unit is in a separate building from the main office. The Director hasn't visited our location in two years."

---

19. Lipman, Victor. "66% Of Employees Would Quit If They Feel Unappreciated." *Forbes*, April 15, 2017. Accessed April 15, 2017. https://www.forbes.com/sites/victorlipman/2017/04/15/66-of-employees-would-quit-if-they-feel-unappreciated/?sh=a7c581c68979.

"My boss's office is down the hall. She forgot I worked in the same hall. I've worked here six months."

"My supervisor keeps calling me Jennifer. I go by Jenny. I've worked here five years."

"My boss hasn't talked to me in four months. I'm remote. I think he forgot he hired me (I was hired remotely)."

"I was on a planning committee for six months with our Vice President in face-to-face meetings. The other day she introduced herself like we had never met."

"My lead assigned me a project that I've been working on for two weeks. When I submitted my work he said, *"Oh yeah, sorry we decided to go in a different direction. We don't need this."*

"Why should I say anything? It's not like anyone around here even knows or cares what I do."

All these statements are ones that I have heard from real people in real work situations who are experiencing real examples of feeling ignored or undervalued. Some I've said myself. When we are acknowledged, even if it is brief, we feel connected to the other

LEADERSHIP IS AN INTENTIONAL INTERPERSONAL RELATIONSHIP

person and to our environment. When we are not acknowledged we feel disconnected which can lead to various negative outcomes.

Acknowledgment is one of the most basic forms of human interaction. It's about saying, "Hello, fellow human. I see you; I know who you are; I acknowledge that you are part of the team."

Leadership is an interpersonal relationship. To establish the connection with the other person while looking through the lens of the Door Holder, we must own that the connection with the other person is an *intentional* interpersonal relationship. This is where the role of the Door Holder can establish meaningful professional connections simply through our communication and actions.

The key to the question is the word intentionality. Just as in the story of my direct report, Claudia, asking why I hated her, I wasn't intending to send that message, but sadly that was the message received. It may not be intended to convey that a Leader doesn't care about employees' ideas, but this may occur without an awareness of the intentionality of our actions.

I shared that I have a background in interpersonal communication, so allow me to provide a bit of Communication 101. Every communication interaction has a sender and a receiver. The sender sends a message; this could be **YOU CANNOT NOT COMMUNICATE** spoken, nonverbal, or in these examples from above, the sender is sending nothing, so silence. The receiver (the team member) gets the message and interprets it. The meaning of the message ultimately lies with the receiver. If there is an open two-way communication channel, the message can get bounced back and forth between the sender and receiver until mutual understanding occurs. As with Claudia, we went back to my office and had a two-hour long conversation to make sure each other was on the same page. But in the previous examples there is simply no communication channel or if there is one, it is inefficient.

We cannot always control the interpretation of the message, but we can control when there is an absence of communication (or closed communication channel). When there is an absence of communication, the void will be filled with the receiver's meaning. If you are sending messages (intentional or not) that could be interpreted as though you don't care, don't know who your employees are, or are uninterested in the work and effort they produce, then in that receiver's mind, you are *not* acknowledging that person.

You must be intentional about the communication you are sending or not sending. And you must remember this golden rule of communication, "You cannot NOT communicate."

We take for granted how our words and actions send messages. We get wrapped up in the right words to say when sometimes it's our actions that scream the loudest. Olivia said all the right words, but her actions didn't match.

Nonverbal communication comprises around 65-75% of all our communication.[20] When most people think of nonverbal communication, they think of facial expressions or body language. But communication that allows for the most receiver interpretation is silence.

What if you came to several blank pages as you read this book? I'm not saying anything, there are no words, but your mind would still create all types of scenarios. You would fill in the void with meaning.

---

20. Griffin, Emory A. *A First Look at Communication Theory.* New York: McGraw-Hill, 1997.

How many times have you sent a text message and there is no response? What do you do? You fill in the blank with your own meaning. *They didn't get the message. They are busy. Their phone is dead. They are mad at me. They were in an accident.* And the list goes on.

Why? Because silence or lack of communication allows the receiver to create any message they want. Is the meaning always negative? That depends on the climate, which we will discuss in a later chapter.

Nonverbal communication is more meaningful than spoken words and it is more believable. We need to look at the idea of silence in a broader sense. Silence can also mean the absence of, or the ignoring of something.

For example, in the quote, *"My supervisor keeps calling me Jennifer. I go by Jenny,"* the supervisor could give Jenny countless accolades, but they boil down to words with no meaning if the incorrect name is constantly used. In this example, the silence comes from completely ignoring (or being silent) the name Jenny prefers. It sends the message that Jenny is just a cog in the wheel, that her identity is her job. It sends the message the supervisor doesn't care enough to remember her name and what she prefers to be called.

This is also true of employees who may have a name that is harder to pronounce, which is reduced to something easy for others to say. Speaking from experience as someone who uses her middle name and has a name that is sometimes confusing to pronounce correctly, I notice when people are trying to acknowledge and know me.

Acknowledgment is a powerful tool, more powerful than most people realize. It is also very easily ignored when things get busy.

YES! YOU BELONG HERE! (ACKNOWLEDGMENT)

Sense of belonging is a term that is used frequently. We want work environments that are inclusive and where employees feel they belong. This increases productivity, collaboration, and retention.

Creating a sense of belonging doesn't have to be a lavish display or immensely time-consuming. In the summer of 2022, I attended my first National Speaker Association Influence conference. I had been speaking for years but never knew this organization existed. My excitement was tempered with a thick layer of intimidation. I didn't know anyone, and self-doubt that I was even qualified to be there started kicking in.

When I arrived, I navigated to registration, signed in, and received my swag bag. Turning around, I came face to face with an energetic conference goer who screamed, "Hi, welcome to Influence!"

I must have displayed visible surprise because she raised her hands with palms up like she was approaching a scared animal.

She replied very cautiously, "Oh, I'm sorry; I didn't mean to startle you; I'm Lisa, from Wisconsin."

I echoed, "I'm Cié from San Antonio."

We chatted about my first time at the conference, and she answered my questions. Then we went our separate ways. The next day when I was at dinner with my family (who had accompanied me), she got seated next to us. Hundreds of people were at this conference, and she said hello to all of them, so I didn't expect her to remember me. But she looked over and said, "Hi, Cié from San Antonio. Is this your family!" She met my family, joked with my extremely shy 14-year-old son, and asked how the conference was going. That's all it took to feel connected to a conference I had never attended where I had no professional connections. That's all it took to make me feel like I belonged. That sense of belonging fueled me to engage with more people and get to know them beyond their name tags. Through this simple acknowledgment, she helped build my Agency, which allowed me to manage any intimidation I felt. By this tiny act, she was a Door Holder. Thanks, Lisa from Wisconsin.

Lisa opened the Door to a phenomenon that helps create effective teams and belonging. When Lisa introduced herself and later remembered me and was genuinely interested in me beyond a conference attendee, she began cultivating a sense of social belonging. Once I felt like I belonged in that space, my Agency grew, and I made even more connections.

Social belonging is a fundamental human need. Cultivating a sense of social belonging at work helps create a positive environment with purpose, connection, and acknowledgment.

Employees feel they belong if:
- They are known by the organization, and their work and effort is acknowledged as being valuable.

- They believe that Leadership cares enough to invest in their growth.
- They are provided professional development opportunities, training, and inquiries into their passions and interests.
- They are asked about their desired career trajectory.
- They are empowered to provide feedback in honest, non-threatening, nonjudgmental conversations where positive intent is assumed.
- They can bring their whole selves to work in an inclusive and accepting environment.
- They can trust that Leadership will have their back and that they are part of a team.

We acknowledged the need for a welcoming environment where people know your name and make you feel like an integral part of the team; now, let's take it a step further and find some common ground that can foster this sense of belonging.

WE HAVE SOMETHING IN COMMON!

All humans are inherently social creatures. Although the depth varies from person to person, we desire to be connected in some way to those we work with.

The process of social interaction includes social rules that we all adhere to. For example, Lisa progressed through the accepted norms of greeting someone. As humans, we get to know one another gradually by sharing information. As a relationship develops, we generally move along a scale of self-disclosure depending on the nature of the relationship.

For example, when we first meet someone, it is an exchange of generic banter. However, a deeper connection can form if you find a point of common ground or relatability.

You may go to your favorite coffee shop every morning. The barista knows your name and the type of coffee you like. You exchange morning greetings. This generic form of communication suits the purpose of the interaction. However, your co-worker, who you have sat by for ten years, most likely has a deeper form of communication with you. Generally speaking, the deeper the interpersonal communication, the longer the social interaction has occurred. And yes, you may have worked with a coworker for ten years and still be at the barista level, depending on many factors.

This can vary not only by depth but also by breadth. Maybe you only know that Francine hates olives, but with Maria, you know she likes to bake and has career goals of becoming a director to better support her family.

You don't need to know deep secrets to reach some common ground. Rather, remember spouse's and children's names, ask about their vacations and weekends, and follow up on a discussion that the employee brought to you or something they showed an interest in.

Regardless of where you are on the social interaction scale with someone, as human beings who are inherently social and need to belong, we seek to reduce uncertainty about those around us because we find uncertainty unpleasant. We are naturally motivated to reduce it.

The reason lack of communication causes the receiver to fill in the void is because we are uncertain about the message, and we don't like that feeling, so we create meaning. This is the process when we get to know someone. Sometimes we unknowingly reduce uncertainty incorrectly by filling in gaps with our false assumptions or biases. It is important to watch out for this.

HIGH SCHOOL FOOTBALL

When I was new to the professional field, I was experiencing friction with an employee from another office named Beth. I had to work closely with Beth on projects that required problem-solving and collaboration. Nothing obviously negative presented itself, but interactions were awkward, with stifled dialogue and uncomfortable silence. The first reason for this odd relationship was the rhetoric about Beth's office that was shared with me. I was told her office was difficult and rigid. So, inexperienced me generalized this trait to everyone in that office. The

> **FINDING COMMON GROUND TAKES SOME OF THE MYSTERY OUT OF HUMAN INTERACTIONS.**

second reason was that Beth's and my personality differed greatly. I was loud and hyper; she was quiet and reserved. Therefore, with every interaction, I only chose to view her from the script I was given and take any uncomfortableness as further validation of 'difficult and rigid.'

Our office hosted a lunch event, and Beth shared my desk to eat. At first, I was annoyed because of our history of uneasiness. Then, we started talking. We discovered that we went to neighboring small-town Texas high schools that played each other in football; we even graduated just a few years apart. I talked about how I was the twirler, and she talked about being in the band. Suddenly, we found a connection, some common ground. You may not believe it, but that's all it took for our relationship to become solid, productive, and congenial.

Finding common ground takes some of the mystery out of human interactions. It displaces any 'us versus them' mentality because if you have a connection, that person is no longer a 'them.'

Understanding where someone is coming from is a powerful diffuser of everyday annoyances. Even though we only connected on this tiny level, I suddenly felt less annoyed and started re-evaluating my misconceptions. Since we had this in common, we seemed more similar, and it was easier for me to look at things from Beth's point of view. Rather than jumping to the negative, I found myself thinking, *"Maybe she asked for more data because she is trying to avoid an audit,"* instead of, *"She thinks I'm doing it wrong; she's so difficult and rigid!"*

Agency means holding the Door open to write your own script about those you enter relationships with. I had failed to form my own opinion. It took Agency to move away from that mindset and even more Agency to knock down negative and unproductive comments from those who had deemed Beth and her team 'them'.

Professional connection in a team is important because it allows you to understand your employees. Another added benefit is that issues can be identified faster because there is a rapport with staff. You can see when something is off, even by having a small connection with someone. You may be thinking, *"I go to work to work, not to make friends."* That's fair; I'm not advocating for friendships (although that can be a lovely by-product of finding connections).

There can be ramifications if you don't have any relationships or interpersonal understandings with the people you work with. You won't recognize their behavioral traits. For example, we have all received spam and phishing emails that seem authentic. In one case, a phishing scam came across my office's email, sent to all my team, stating I had shared a document with them. The instructions were to open immediately because it needed urgent attention. Several of my team asked if it was legitimate because they knew I didn't share documents in this manner, nor would I demand anything in that tone. They knew me and had the Agency to stop and say, "*Wait, something is off.*" They had the Agency to manage the outcomes because uncertainty was low.

On the contrary, I had a colleague, Nicole, who unfortunately lacked this basic familiarity with her boss. Her work environment was one in which she barely knew her leader, only conversing occasionally and meetings were quick. Nicole was having personal issues that were impacting her focus at work but she had no idea how her boss would react to personal challenges, so she kept the information to herself and forged ahead. Late one afternoon, Nicole received an urgent email about paying a vendor that looked like it was from her boss. She didn't have the Agency to say, "*Wait, something is off*" and sent $5,000 to a scammer.

One-on-one connections remove some ambiguity and uncertainty we are all trying to remedy in our relationships. Seeing individuals for who they are, beyond their job function, is valuable. How do you ensure this is happening? The most basic way of starting and maintaining those connections is to establish and keep that one-on-one regular meeting.

THE TWO WAY ONE-ON-ONE

Research from Gallup indicates that employees who have regular meetings with their managers are three times as likely to be engaged as those who don't.[21] The one-on-one meeting holds more power than some may think.

I know the positive impact intentional one-on-one meetings with one's supervisor has on employee morale and motivation. I only realized how important it was once I switched positions and had a very uninterested supervisor who canceled most of our one-on-ones because something else always came up.

> **THE ONE-ON-ONE MEETING BUILDS TRUST BOTH WAYS**

The effectiveness of the one-on-one meeting comes from the conversation that is had, not symbolically being on the calendar. As you recall, Leadership is an intentional interpersonal relationship which means the one-on-one is not only a time to catch up on what's happening progress-wise but also a time to invest in attention to that team member specifically. It opens that critical communication channel that can allow for the bouncing back and forth of messages to achieve mutual understanding. Investment of your time builds Agency and holds the Door. The one-on-one builds trust both ways between the supervisor and employee. If Leaders don't in-

---

21 Mann, Annamarie, and Ryan Darby. "Should Managers Focus on Performance or Engagement?" *Gallup Business Journal*, August 5, 2014. Accessed August 5, 2014. https://news.gallup.com/businessjournal/174197/managers-focus-performance-engagement.aspx.

vest time in their team, how can they ask their team to invest time in the organization?

Below are some tips to remember when creating this opportunity to connect through the one-on-one meeting.

- **Please don't cancel.** Imagine this is your situation. Your meetings with your supervisor have been canceled without rescheduling for the last four months. You had agenda items to discuss, and your boss knew this. How does this make you feel? Not very valued. What message are you filling the void with? As a Leader, it is your responsibility to schedule recurring one-on-ones, and if there must be a cancelation, reschedule it. If you are a chronic canceler of one-on-ones, reflect on the message it sends to the team.
- **Set and maintain boundaries.** One-on-one meetings are about developing trusting professional relationships, setting goals for professional work, and solving any obstacles that get in the way of this work. It is not about gossiping or always being a sounding board for constant complaints. Listen to issues but ask for solutions instead of trying to solve or fix them yourself. Empower your staff with the decision-making ability to solve issues or at least come to you with ideas for solutions. Make it known that tearing others down, or spreading conspiracy theories, is never on the agenda.
- **At LEAST once a quarter, talk about something other than work**. Ask about their life, their favorite show, or their cat. Share something about yourself on an equal level. The depth of relationships will vary from person to person. It is obvious when someone is in-

terested in you as a professional and when someone is just faking it. Author Kim Scott of *Radical Candor* states, "it's more than about being a professional, it's about giving a damn, sharing more than just your work self, and encouraging everyone who reports to you to do the same." (p. 9)[22]

- **Inquire about growth**. Ask about their professional goals, their ambitions, what's going well, and what's not going well in terms of employment satisfaction. Be ready for feedback that may require some action or reflection.
- **Dig Deeper**. Don't stop the meeting early because you run out of things to say or want to gain an extra fifteen minutes to work on something else. Use this time to make a deeper connection or explore areas of the individual's professional interest. Take this extra time to ask, "How are you doing?" and when they say, "Fine," follow it with, "How are you *really* doing?" The answers will surprise you. I've also noticed that sometimes when I ask this question, the team member begins a blow-by-blow of their daily activities. I stop them and say, "I know your productivity; I'm asking how you as a person are doing." This is not asking for private details of their lives, but rather is a good way to check for burnout, low morale, or concerns about something they may not know is okay to discuss. You must open the Door to allow for honest feedback. Everything will only sometimes be 'fine.'

---

22. Scott, Kim. *Radical Candor: How to Get What You Want by Saying What You Mean.* New York: St. Martin's Press, 2017, 9.

- **Recognize unexpected power dynamics.** My office is in the 'executive' building, while my team is across campus. I was holding one-on-ones in my office. One day when I was across campus visiting one of the team's centers, I overheard some staff talking about the building I was in and how they hated going over there. I asked why they felt this way. They stated there are too many Executives up there, and the building is like the principal's office. It had never occurred to me that a space might create apprehension and thus limit the flow of information. So, now I go to their spaces so conversations feel more comfortable and relaxed. This also gives me time to casually interact with the team.
- **Never multi-task in a one-on-one.** All your attention should be on the person, not your phone, email, or any other distraction. And yes, everyone can tell when you are trying to subtly check your email. Valuable information can be missed if your attention is elsewhere. If someone knows you aren't listening, why would they bother sharing something?

From the basic recognition of being part of the team, to finding common ground and fostering a sense of belonging, to that important one-on-one connection that can make work interactions more fluid and collaborative, acknowledgment is a powerful tool in creating Agency.

> "Communication is merely an exchange of information, but connection is an exchange of our humanity."
>
> – *Sean Stephenson*

THOUGHTS TO CONSIDER

- People will leave if they feel invisible, ignored, or unappreciated.
- Leadership is about establishing and maintaining intentional interpersonal relationships.
- Silence is a powerful form of communication. Meaning will be made to fill the void.
- Uncertainty makes us uncomfortable.
- Acknowledgment creates a sense of belonging.
- No matter how different you think you are from someone, you can always find common ground.
- Be your authentic self, even if this means vulnerability.
- One-on-one connections foster trust.
- Make sure you are connecting with everyone, not just the ones easy to connect with.
- Be intentionally curious, intentionally reflect on interactions.

Chapter 3

G IS FOR GROWTH

"A Leader's job is not to do the work for others, it's to help others figure out how to do it themselves, to get things done, and to succeed beyond what they thought possible."

— SIMON SINEK

THE WHINY CROSSFITTER

When I completed my doctorate, I was filled with a solid sense of academic achievement, but I felt terrible physically. I had excelled intellectually but failed miserably by letting my health slide down the priority list in favor of good grades. I am self-aware enough to know that I will not stick with a healthy plan unless I'm held accountable in some way. Fortunately, after three years of a coworker pitching her exercise regimen to me, I finally decided to sign up for CrossFit.

I'll admit, I thought that if I signed up, and proudly told people I was a CrossFitter suddenly I would morph into this fit athletic version of myself. I would be Dr. CrossFit!

After about six months into my CrossFit journey, I found myself at the end of an exceptionally challenging workout. Feeling frustrated and disheartened, I walked up to the coach and said in my most whiny and pathetic voice, "Hey, can I talk to you?" I began my lamenting:

ME: "Coach, I'm not getting any better. I don't have a lot of stamina. I get winded when I run. I'm not lifting any heavier. I just feel like I'm not making any progress. Do you have any advice?"

The coach looked me dead in the eye.

COACH: "How many days a week are you coming? Like two? Yeah, it's two because I'm here all the time and you aren't. How is your nutrition? Are you eating junk food? What did you have for lunch?"

ME: ... *a hamburger with fries and a Dr. Pepper.*

COACH: "What's your water intake like? Are you drinking alcohol? Are you pushing your weightlifting during class or doing what's comfortable? You've been coming for six months, and you are still lifting the same as when you started. Are you running at home to build endurance or only doing it here when you show up one day a week?"

ME: *Wow, ok this is not what I expected.*

COACH: "What are you doing to improve yourself?"

Feeling a bit overwhelmed, I pondered my own actions:

What am I really doing? I joined CrossFit, so that should be the magic wand to physical fitness, right? Similarly, in the self-help area, we have all acquired books on certain subjects, like Leadership, so just holding it or displaying it on the shelf should solve all our Leadership problems, right? We should be Dr. Leadership, right? Yeah, see where this is going?

I went home mad. I decided that next class I would give it my all.

The only time I could work out was in the afternoons, and I live in Texas. It was summer, 100 degrees with high humidity. But regardless of the weather, today was the day I was going to give it everything I had. I hate running and I hate burpees, and the workout was running and burpees.

Sigh, I got this, let's go.

First round, I'm maintaining, but on the uphill run I solidified my usual position of dead last.

Second round, I'm not ok. Breathing is difficult and I'm getting lapped by the other runners.

Third round, I'm drenched in sweat, it's in my eyes, and my throat hurts from the deep breaths I'm forced to take. Now my burpees have turned into me falling to the ground and getting back up, and my running has turned into something akin to a zombie movie. Then it started.

Have you ever fainted? It begins with a black fog that creeps in from the sides of your eyes before everything goes black. As I was running, I started seeing the black fill in. For context (because this is important), I'm at the far end of the run in a sparsely populated industrial park that backs up to the woods. I frequently see deer and random coyotes in the vicinity. I think, *if I faint, no one will know for at least twenty minutes. Everyone else is finished, and they know how slow I am. I'm out of eyesight of the building so I'll just lay here until someone starts to wonder. I'll probably get hauled off by a couple of coyotes.*

The black was getting worse. It was all I could focus on. My heart was racing, and my fear of faint was increasing. I pushed myself up the hill and back into the workout space. Convinced I was going to drop to the ground at any moment, I rushed to the bathroom to cool off.

Before I cupped water in my hands to splash my face, I looked in the mirror to assess signs of imminent collapse. That's when I saw it.

On my face, right below my right eye was a tiny black *thing*. I had to get an inch away from the mirror to see it. It was a piece of the floor from one of the black rubber mats. It had gotten stuck to my sweaty face doing burpees. That's what I was seeing, the black shadow, the impending faint, the fear. There was *nothing* physically wrong with me; it was a **piece of floor** stuck to my face.

I walked into the workout that day with a surface level determination to succeed, but with a rooted assumption that I was probably going to fail. I was so focused on accepting any sign that I was failing, I grabbed the first negative thing I could find and let it morph into something terrifying. The terrifying negativity turned out to not even be real, it was a manifestation of my own self-doubts and unwillingness to accept that I had the

> **SOMETIMES GROWTH MEANS TAKING A HARD LOOK IN THE MIRROR**

ability. I needed to push myself and be uncomfortable to reach the growth. If I had never looked in the mirror, I might have never discovered that tiny little piece of floor that was causing all the drama.

Sometimes growth means taking a hard look in the mirror. Sometimes we only look because someone has forced us to. Admitting that we aren't trying our best or admitting we are holding on to false pieces of floor is difficult.

When have you taken a hard look at yourself as a Leader? When have you challenged your staff with growth the way my coach challenged me? Who in your organization (including you) is walking around with a piece of floor on their face?

If we as Leaders hope to grow others, we must assess what holds people back.

- Sometimes we keep ourselves from growing by placing imaginary limits we think we can't change.
- Sometimes we cozy up with complacency and never want to move.
- Sometimes we think that success should come just because we take the first small shuffle toward it.
- Sometimes we think a label or a title means growth.
- Sometimes we think that the power of our decision alone to make a change is enough to make things suddenly happen without putting in the work.

My coach knew I was capable of more than I was giving. When I complained about my progress, he didn't lament with me, he got specific and real on what I was not doing to grow. He sent texts if I missed too many workouts and made the effort to understand who I was beyond another number on his client list. Although his words initially made me mad, I realized he cared about my progress. He is a Door Holder and gives me the Agency to know I can make a change if I put the work into it. Thanks Coach.

We have the Agency to pick the piece of floor off our face and grow into the Leaders we were meant to be. We have the ability to hold the Door, and to help others do this as well.

Being a Door Holder means pushing people along, showing them the reality of their skills, talents, potential and developing a growth mindset.

You may be thinking, "Hold on, I thought all I had to do was hold the Door open for the people I've acknowledged and connected with. Now I must push them through?" No, you must cultivate them into being prepared to walk through the Door. This chapter is about growing those in your line so when you hold the Door they are ready.

As you read this chapter, I want you to think about that team member that you have deemed extremely difficult. If we are honest with ourselves, we can identify times in the past where we have shut the Door on individuals because of personality differences, conscious or unconscious biases, or just because it seemed they were too dang contrary. Chapter 4 explores empathy and seeking to understand. Therefore, if you have someone, or a group of someones in mind as we navigate growth together, you can slide into the empathy chapter well prepared to change your mindset. Speaking of mindset, let's explore growth versus fixed mindsets.

CONCRETE BUNKERS OR FERTILE FIELDS

Psychologist Carol Dweck[23] asserts that intelligence, talent, or even education isn't what sets people apart, it's their mindset and the way they approach life's challenges. Agency is your belief that you can approach life's trials and manage whatever the outcome may be. Having Agency is having a growth mindset. I can learn about CrossFit, read books, or watch documentaries, but it's the mindset that will actually make me improve. As my story illustrated, I was met with challenges and obstacles, and pushed out of my comfort zone. The piece of floor on my face was enforcing a fixed mindset that my ability was at the limit. You can read 100 books about Leadership and tools, techniques, and philosophies to adopt to be a better Leader, but it's your mindset that will make the difference. You can read this book with a desire to be intentional, get messy, and face challenges, or you can say, "Well that's nice, but I think I'll just keep doing it the way it's always been done."

To be a Door Holder, you need to create an environment that is growth minded, where trust, empowerment, ownership, and motivation to improve thrive. And you need to be growth minded to make this happen.

We will talk about self-doubt and confidence issues in Chapter 6, but I think we can all agree that the desire to look like we have it all together is immense. Especially if you are in a Leadership position – whether that has been deemed by title or informally. We become trapped in our fixed mindsets

---

23. Dweck, Carol S. Mindset: *The New Psychology of Success*. New York: Ballantine Books, 2007.

if we are so wrapped up in appearing perfect that we avoid anything that might shake that. My fixed mindset in CrossFit (piece of floor on my face) was causing me to want to give up and feel my effort was useless. Why should I even try?

Looking at fixed and growth a different way. A fixed mindset is a concrete bunker. The information that is in there is sealed up, safe and sound, and there is no way anything new is going to penetrate it. But the growth mind is like a fertile field, welcoming new growth. It's dynamic and can adapt to change. Which type of team looks better to you, a bunch of concrete bunkers, or a vibrant green field?

If we live in a fixed mindset, we are also more likely to fester in jealousy or be threatened by other's success. Their success makes us look less smart, less competent, less perfect. Living in a fixed state where you give up easily, avoid challenges, and are always threatened by other's successes does not make a Door Holder. And if you are opposed to challenges and changes, you will never walk through the Door.

Having a fixed mindset doesn't always mean giving up when things get tough or thinking you don't have the ability to do something. It can also be a fixed belief you already know everything there is to know about something. If you believe you already know everything, no new information will be allowed to penetrate your concrete bunker.

> **NOTHING GROWS OUT OF CONCRETE**

Leadership is messy – it's a journey. That's the essence of having a growth mindset. That fertile field will get messy, while that concrete bunker may stay clean. But nothing grows out of concrete. Our Leadership intelligence can be cultivated as we learn through experience. Nothing taught me more about the fact that I will never stop learning about Leadership like the pandemic. Suddenly I didn't have answers to questions, the future was uncertain, and challenges in my professional world were numerous. It doesn't have to be something as traumatic as a pandemic to disrupt our Leadership flow. Mandated layoffs, high employee turnover, new Leadership, changes in regulations, changes in funding, that problem employee that is untouchable because of 'politics,' there are always peaks and valleys. We never get to a nirvana of Leadership knowledge because the world changes around us, new generations enter the workforce with new perspectives, and (hopefully) your industry changes and evolves. Leadership requires a growth mindset. As with a fertile field, there will be the planting season and the harvest, the rains and drought, but there is always new growth.

> **WE NEVER GET TO A NIRVANA OF LEADERSHIP KNOWLEDGE BECAUSE THE WORLD CHANGES AROUND US**

Fixed Mindset	Growth Mindset
Avoid anything challenging or hard	Challenges are accepted
Tendency to give up when encountering obstacles	Obstacles are expected and embraced
Feedback is ignored or avoided	Feedback is sought after
Effort is useless	Effort achieves results
Success of others is threatening	Success of others is inspiring
Marinates in failure	Learns from failure
Believes intelligence is static	Intelligence is malleable

Adapted from Dweck

Agency grows in that field of a growth mindset environment. People who have a growth mindset are more likely to state their honest opinions and openly express their disagreements when communicating. On the contrary, fixed mindset people tend to be concerned about being perceived as smart and let their anxiety about disapproval for their ideas thwart productive discussion.[24]

As a Leader, having the right conversations about growth will benefit not only your employees but you as a Leader too. One of the best ways to encourage growth is through praise. Praise can contribute to building a growth mindset,

---

24. Dweck, "Mindset"

but it needs to be provided in a specific and effective manner. When giving praise to encourage a growth mindset, it's important to focus on the process, effort, strategies, and perseverance that an individual puts into their work, rather than solely on their innate talent or outcome. It also must be authentic and tailored to the individual. You know how to foster a connection, the rest of this chapter will explore growth through praise and constructive criticism.

GOLDILOCKS PRAISE

Praise is a tricky subject. Some people love it or even need it, and others do not. Some get excited over lavish public displays of praise, and others prefer quiet one-on-one acknowledgment. Think about yourself for a moment; if you just completed a long project and were being praised for your efforts, which type of praise would you prefer:

1. Being called up to a stage in front of your entire company and asked to give a speech on the success of the project.
2. Your Leadership sent emails of praise, noting the specifics of what you did well.
3. A small office party with the team who worked on the project with you.
4. A monetary bonus.
5. Nothing at all because you were just doing your job.

Praise validates that all your hard work means something. Praise validates that the time, thought, effort, focus, and sometimes sweat and tears were not in vain. Even if the goal was not met, the effort is commendable. Praising for effort has more influence than praising for performance.[25] A growth mindset values the effort that is required to tackle any challenge or obstacle.

Agency, specifically self-efficacy (belief in your ability to perform in situations), can be influenced by encouragement about an individual's performance.[26] Praise increases self-esteem, motivation and conveys to the person their ability. However, an abundance of praise isn't always the answer. Too much praise can be negative. It becomes noise especially if it lacks specificity or is thrown at anyone regardless of the effort they may put forth. Yet no praise at all can have serious effects. It's like the nursery rhyme Goldie Locks and the Three Bears – not too hot, not too cold, but how do you determine what is just right?

Before we begin, reflect more about how you handle praise. It is important to understand your personal preferences and also understand that your preferences are not universal. We cannot always approach others the same way we prefer to be approached when it comes to praise. How would you answer these questions.

1. How do I feel about praise?
2. Do I like public or private praise?
3. When I receive praise I most often feel_____.
4. What are my strengths and how do I like to be recognized for them?

---

25. Dweck, "Mindset"
26. Redmond, Brian F. "Self-Efficacy Theory: Do I Think That I Can Succeed in My Work? Work Attitudes and Motivation." *The Pennsylvania State University, World Campus*, 2010.

5. What do I value most? Recognition for my personal qualities such as being on time, being a team player, loyalty, or task qualities like knowledge in a certain topic, ability to do a skill (like coding or budgeting)? Why do I value one more?
6. Even if I didn't reach the desired outcome, is praise for my effort beneficial?
7. Does everyone on my team like to receive praise the same way? Why or why not? How do I know this?

BAH HUMBUG

When I was in college, I worked at a fancy clothing store in the fancy part of town. The pay was barely minimum wage, with a discount on clothing serving as an additional benefit. The store manager was understanding, patient, and forgiving of mistakes (I made a lot of mistakes). She saw every stumble as a chance to learn and praised my effort. The entire staff worked hard because she was so encouraging and motivating. We were young and inexperienced, and she held the Door for us to grow.

The owner of the store was the opposite of the manager. Disorganized, impatient, and constantly watching for us to do something wrong. The climate changed the moment she entered the store; it was like she entered with storm clouds and lightning creating a thick electricity in the air.

It was the holiday season, our busiest time. The owner gave us a lofty sales goal to close out the year with a good profit margin. As a team, and with the encouragement of the manager, we met it ahead of schedule.

On Christmas Eve, expecting a lot of last-minute shoppers, another employee and I arrived early to open the store. As I was stocking the tissue paper, my coworker screamed from the back room that our mail cubbies were stuffed with fat envelopes. Hopeful anticipation erupted as we grabbed the envelopes, excited for a holiday surprise, or dare I say, a bonus from exceeding the sales goal early. Ripping open the envelopes with the fervor of children on Christmas morning, the giggles slowly disappeared. It was not a gift, not even a Christmas card. It was a list from the owner of the store detailing everything we did wrong that year and what we needed to improve upon for next. It was *ten* pages long. There was no "Merry Christmas" or "Thank you" or mention of how we exceeded the sales goal. No appreciation. I quit that January.

We weren't expecting to find a large bundle of cash, but knowing how hard we worked and that our work helped the owner meet her financial obligations to the store created an expectation of at least some form of appreciation or acknowledgment. And I should note this was only one example of a toxic environment, this was just the final straw.

Praise doesn't have to be something over the top. But it must be given in a specific and sincere way.

S^2 SPECIFICITY AND SINCERITY

As you explore 'too hot' and 'too cold' praise and learn how your team receives praise in the most meaningful way, start with the two foundations of praise that will always apply: being specific and sincere.

We all need to move away from statements like "good job, everyone" or "nice work." Those types of statements are general and not specific. Yes, they are acknowledgments, but we can try a little harder to make our praise more meaningful. We can all be more intentional in our communication (reducing uncertainty) by being more specific. Here is an example:

Pretend you have just organized a large stakeholder event. Which two options of praise have more meaning?

Option A: Good job, Keep up the good work!

Option B: Cié, good job on organizing last night's stakeholder event. Because of your attention to detail and prior planning, the event ran smoothly. Your event management skills are top-notch, and I know you put a lot of effort into this program. Keep up the good work.

Which would you prefer?

I chose Option B.

First, they used my name, which goes back to acknowledgment. Second, it was specific, about what I did well,

BEING SPECIFIC ABOUT PRAISE REDUCES UNCERTAINTY AND AMBIGUITY

and when it was performed. Third, a value identifier was added about my ability to plan ahead and pay attention to detail. This is effective because now I'm on the same page of the praise book as the person sending the message. There is clarity in what was deemed valuable. My Agency around stakeholder event planning is increased. My growth mindset around my ability has increased. I'm much more likely to feel I can tackle challenges if they arise at the next stakeholder event I manage.

Be open to the idea that people may make different connections than you. If I had only received the praise of generic 'good job', I may have thought 'good job' meant it was good because a lot of people came, or the food was tasty. Being specific reduces uncertainty and ambiguity. And as you know, we are always trying to reduce uncertainty. Be specific and clear so the receiver doesn't fill the void with their own meaning.

The second part is being sincere. Trust me from experience, it is very easy to tell when someone is just saying 'good job' and there is no sincerity behind it.

Flashback to when I was a mere twenty-three-years-old and teaching high school English. It was book report day, and an incredibly intelligent student was presenting his report to the class. He was always prepared and delivered top-quality work. Probably because I knew he would do well, I unconsciously allowed my mind to wander as he was speaking. Suddenly, the class was clapping, and I snapped back to reality realizing I hadn't listened to a single word he said. I said what I have just told you not to say,

"Good job, keep up the good work".

He replied, "Thank you", then he paused and asked,

"I'd like to know what you thought was good and what feedback you have Mrs. Gee."

He knew I wasn't being sincere.

There are two lessons from this. First, we sometimes fall into an automatic expectation with our star performers. We know they will do well, so we fail to pay attention or focus on their performance. Then we are left with nothing but the generic 'good job'. Second, if we are being sincere, we should choose honesty. I should have apologized that I spaced out and wasn't paying attention. Is that being vulnerable? Yes, but authenticity is more important than trying to fake your way through.

Sincerity also means being honest if praise is not required. If the event, project, presentation, or job went poorly, you need to be honest. If the effort displayed was lackluster, you need to explain why you felt it was subpar. We will discuss constructive criticism later, but first let's explore some tips for giving praise.

Don't wait for grandeur. Does Janice always take the time to organize the calendar? Does Juan answer the phone or Zoom call with a smile and positive attitude even in chaotic times? Does Kevin water the office plants? Offer appreciation for the small things too. Offer praise for the effort people are making to improve their office, the work culture, or themselves.

Don't overlook the underachievers. By underachievers, I mean the ones still learning or adjusting to a new role or new duty, not the slackers. Praise is a motivator, and you can always find something praiseworthy to recognize so people know when they are on the right path. Recognize their diligence in learning, recognize their trials, errors, and growth. Recognize that you believe they can succeed. Some of the most valuable praise I have received is when I failed, or when the situation went grossly askew, but I handled it with grace, tact, and professionalism. I was praised for my composure and effort during an unsuccessful situation.

Paise someone who isn't there. If you feel awkward about giving praise to a person, then spread it around to others and lift that person up, it will get back to them. This type of interaction builds trust and a climate of appreciation. Create a culture where people commonly praise the good work of others on their team.

Don't allow gossip to trump praise. If you find yourself tearing people down or always finding fault, recalibrate. Environments that allow gossip to run freely are tainted soil where Agency will not grow. Changing the culture of spreading rumors takes Agency. If rumors are an issue in your area, perhaps you need to revisit your communication. Are you being transparent enough or communicating enough with staff (this includes listening), so they do not fill the void with their own meaning, which in this case, turns out to be rumors?

Standing up against gossip and those who enjoy wallowing in it, means you may lose some work 'friends' because you refuse to live in their Judgement Land. I recall an instance of going to lunch with a long-time coworker. The moment we sat down she wanted to know all the gossip. I simply said, "I don't really have any" and proceeded to talk about all the good things that people were doing. Nothing douses the flame of gossip like throwing in a positive comment. Try it.

Don't come on too strong at first. If you suddenly slather everyone with lavish praise, people will think something is wrong, like you are preparing them for bad news. Start small, especially if you have been stingy with praise in the past.

Be honest. I have called myself out before stating,

"I know I'm not good at giving the praise I should. I need you to understand how much I value you as a team member and this is why."

If you are not used to giving praise you will need to learn how to implement it. People will be wondering about the change in you and not listening to your praise.

Don't over-praise. Overwatering plants causes roots to grow shallow, therefore when there is a drought, the roots aren't deep, and the tree suffers. Over-praising and ignoring areas of growth will not make strong roots; they will be shallow and at the first gust of wind, the tree is blown over.

Speaking of ignoring areas of needed growth, let's discuss constructive feedback.

HUMPTY DUMPTY CRITICISM

A growth mindset is easier when things are going well and efforts are commendable. However, there will always be times for constructive feedback, and sometimes there is the need for hard, honest criticism. It is in these moments that the value of a growth mindset becomes critical.

Fixed mindsets don't like criticism or feedback as it may damage their perception of intelligence. Like the nursery rhyme *Humpty Dumpty*, we aim to provide constructive criticism without causing anyone to break, making it difficult to put them back together again. Fixed mindsets could see any acknowledgment of needed improvement as the ultimate failure. Part of a growth mindset that builds Agency and holds the Door is your belief that you can change your environment. Opening the Door to give and accept constructive feedback is vital.

Perhaps you agree that sometimes we don't like to give constructive feedback because it makes us feel uncomfortable. We have to tell someone what they are doing it wrong, or how they are interacting with the team is causing strife, or their progress on the report is not satisfactory.

Sometimes giving feedback isn't uncomfortable, but the dynamics are. For example, earlier in my career, I had issues with supervising people that were older than I. They had more experience and I felt I didn't have the authority to say anything perceived as negative about their work performance. I didn't want our relationship to fall off the wall and not be able to be put back together again.

I encourage you to explore some perceptions you have about giving constructive feedback. If you are conflict-avoiding, and giving any constructive feedback makes you uncomfortable, let's look at the negative ramifications that can occur from this silence.

GOOD JOB: YOU'RE FIRED!

Nelson had been with his company for ten years. The annual evaluation system had scoring of E for exceptional, S for satisfactory, and N for needs improvement. Nelson had received nothing less than a rating of E each year from his supervisor Henry. However, Nelson was not efficient at his job. Nelson's countless mistakes and to be cleaned up by other staff, some systems were restricted for him to use due to his accidental changes resulting in a domino effect of errors, and he always respectfully declined to learn new processes, stating he was not ready to take on new work.

Nelson was a congenial, loyal employee, always on time, always friendly and cooperative with the team. Henry, his supervisor, didn't want to hurt Nelson's feelings because he was such a nice person. Therefore, he just cleaned up the messes and told Nelson there were small errors that were taken care of but overall, "Good job." When Henry retired, the company moved Nelson to a new supervisor, and suddenly, his evaluations consistently rated as N. Nelson was confused, deflated, and upset.

For ten years, Nelson's supervisor could have been growing Nelson and working on the skills he needed to develop. But Nelson was always told everything was 'fine.' Due to the lack of growth support and Nelson's fixed mindset, he couldn't function under the new supervisor and as a result, Nelson was fired.

How do you open the Door for constructive feedback? There is a right way and a wrong way, let's cover the wrong way first.

YOUR PRAISE SANDWICH HAS EXPIRED

I'm going to make a statement that is contradictory to some advice you may have heard about how to give feedback.

I do not follow the sandwich rule: praise, criticism, praise. Let me explain why.

People use this method to make themselves feel better about delivering an uncomfortable message. As the bearer of negative news, you might feel better serving a praise sandwich because saying something honest and abrupt like, "Nelson, your data entry skills are riddled with errors and people are complaining," makes us feel uncomfortable. Human interaction isn't always going to be warm accolades, but it can be productive without discomfort. Agency means believing in your ability to make a change, and if your employee is underperforming, you need to help them build Agency to make that change by being honest and helpful. That's holding the Door. If Nelson's supervisor had held the Door for growth, Nelson's outcome may have been different.

Let's break down the sandwich idea to help identify why it's not the best choice. Using the sandwich method can have two different outcomes. The team member only hears the praise, or the team member only hears the critique. Let's start with what most likely happened with Nelson, only hearing the praise and ignoring the constructive feedback.

Here is the first piece of bread in our praise sandwich.

> **HENRY:** "Nelson, you are so punctual; thank you for always being ready to go at the start of the day."
>
> **NELSON:** *That makes me happy; I feel appreciated because I do make the effort to get to work early every day!*

Now, the meat of the sandwich.

> **HENRY:** "BUT there have been complaints about your data entry accuracy."
>
> **NELSON:** *Oh wait, what? Am I doing a good job or am I not?*

It's not over; here comes the other piece of bread.

HENRY: "BUT I do appreciate the reports you prepare each month."

NELSON: *Oh great, ok, I'm doing a good job!*

Henry has just served Nelson a confusing sandwich. If this scenario happened over those ten years, perhaps Nelson only heard the praise and glossed over the real issue. Henry, not wanting to upset Nelson, also glossed over the issues. Henry, in his mind, was doing the due diligence of mentioning it to Nelson but failed to get the point across.

In this situation, the supervisor isn't being intentional with communication; they just want to get it out of the way. An inefficient communication channel is present, lacking the back and forth to establish mutual understanding. Uncertainty is high and blanks are filled with the receiver's (Nelson) meaning.

> **WHEN IT COMES TO GROWING ANOTHER PERSON, IT'S NOT ABOUT HOW COMFORTABLE YOU FEEL; IT'S ABOUT GETTING THE RIGHT MEANING ACROSS TO THE INDIVIDUAL SO THEY CAN GROW.**

Now the second interpretation of the praise sandwich is something I've seen personally. It's the opposite of the above scenario. Instead of only hearing the praise and glossing over the need for improvement, a team member will only hear the negative and the praise will be lost. I noticed these negative effects of the sandwich phenomenon with staff who have come from supervisors that try to soften up constructive criticism with a sprinkle of praise. The team member would get uncomfortable when I gave any type of accolade and would start picking apart the praise I had just given trying to find the bad news. They were looking for what they were doing wrong. Finally, I asked,

"What's wrong? I'm just telling you that you did a good job?"

They revealed that in previous situations, there was always a "BUT" following the praise.

Don't mix praise and constructive/growth feedback. Either the praise will be lost, or the constructive feedback will be lost. Make the intentional effort to praise specifically and sincerely and make the intentional effort to provide constructive criticism clearly with concrete examples. When it comes to growing another person, it's not about how comfortable **you** feel; it's about getting the right meaning across to the individual so **they** can grow.

Addressing the need for improvement doesn't have to be uncomfortable. Having a plan makes it easier to hold the Door.

Approach the situation with positive intent. It's easy to assume the negative or nefarious. People get defensive if they perceive we have the wrong motives. Go back and review making connections. Having a connection, even a small one, will allow constructive criticism and the assumption of positive intent to flow more freely.

Be timely. We tend to put things off that make us uncomfortable, but this just delays progress. If an employee is doing something wrong, ignoring the issue will only make it worse (as seen in the case of ignoring Nelson's errors for ten years). This approach hinders the employee's ability to take ownership and responsibility for their actions. How can anyone improve if you don't know what's wrong?

Schedule a time to talk to the employee. This isn't a fly by or an 'oh by the way' casual or last-minute conversation. Discussing important matters should never be postponed until evaluation time. Make a point to reserve time (and enough time) for this important conversation.

Understand what you want from the conversation. Is it for you? For them? The organization? Were you instructed by your lead or someone else to talk to them? Understanding WHY you are having this conversation contextualizes it and will help you prepare.

Recommend specifics. In elementary school, you learned how to write a story. Who, What, Where, When. Apply this to constructive feedback. Going back to Nelson, Henry could have said: "We have received complaints (what) from users (who) that interact with the data you enter into the system (where). The errors are specifically in the first quarter data (when)."

Quantify it. This is very important. How many complaints have been received? Is it one? Twenty? If Nelson's data entry is causing domino effects, what is the extent of this impact, and how is it impacting the workload? Understanding the quantifiable impact of the feedback changes the meaning.

Give examples. The connotation of 'errors' is relative. What is the real issue? Have concrete data, not generic. Errors can mean anything from entering a wrong date, to transposing numbers to blatantly wrong information because of a serious lack of training. In providing constructive feedback, it is important to give specific examples of actions that did not meet expectations. Often, we fail to manage expectations, assuming everyone thinks the same way we do. It's worth repeating: if there is a void of information, people will fill it with their own story.

Establish acceptance criteria. How do you know when something is *done*? We know Leadership is an intentional interpersonal communicative relationship. Many performance issues result from failure to establish acceptance criteria for when something is complete. In Nelson's example, acceptance criteria for entering data may include spot checking for accuracy, but if this has never been communicated to Nelson, he will not be doing this. This creates a situation where Henry and Nelson are operating out of different rule books. Taking the time to clarify the definition of *done* and all the checks and balances that are needed to declare something is done is extremely valuable. If this is documented, having performance discussions is also much easier.

Finally, open the Door for their feedback. This allows for building a plan *together* for improvement.

> **NEVER ASSUME SILENCE IS AGREEMENT.**

In these conversations, never assume silence is agreement. Listen and validate their understanding of the conversation. If someone confides their real feelings on a situation, thank them for feeling secure enough to do so and don't dismiss any emotions that may arise. And always, if emotions are too heated or it is unsafe, stop the conversation and reconvene when heightened emotions are not at the wheel.

Here is a great sample statement of the scenario we have discussed.

Hi Nelson, thanks for making time to meet (acknowledgment). I've received complaints (what) from users (who) that interact with the data you enter in the system (where). The errors are specifically in the first quarter data (when). I've received three (quantify) complaints from staff in the billing department (who) rely on your first quarter data (why). They stated the data was inaccurate and caused a cascading effect of errors that resulted in a significant invoice issue (example). Can you share your knowledge about any issues with the first quarter data? (feedback)

The message is clear, and the receiver knows exactly where the deficit is. And they are allowed to respond in this open communication channel.

IN REVIEW OF CONSTRUCTIVE CRITICISM

1. Have your facts together and ready to go.
2. Specifics, what, who, where, when.
3. Quantifiable examples.
4. Time set aside for feedback and communication.
5. Listen to understand.
6. Build consensus by validating what you understand.
7. Make a plan of improvement.
8. Establish a follow up time with predetermined acceptance criteria (definition of done).

Below are sample statements to assist in growth conversations. Through a growth mindset, you can create an effective environment that welcomes praise and constructive feedback.

Tool	Example Phrase
Ask for understanding	"I would like a few minutes of your time to better understand this issue."
Acknowledge issues	"I understand that your plate has been very full this past month and several deadlines are approaching."
Clarify your position	"The challenge that I have is that I need this information and we have a tight turnaround."
Assume positive intent	"Your work on the budget is always excellent, it's concerning that it seems to be lagging, is there a roadblock that I can help with?"
Have Empathy	"You have run out of sick leave and if you miss any more days, you will not get paid. Can we work together to explore how to make this work better for everyone?"

"A mind that is stretched by a new experience can never go back to its old dimensions."

– OLIVER WENDELL HOLMES

THOUGHTS TO CONSIDER

- Agency flourishes in a growth mindset environment.
- Growing anything takes time and patience.
- False beliefs (or pieces of floor) can keep us from reaching our true potential.
- Being a Door Holder means pushing people along, showing them the reality of their skills and talents.
- Being specific with praise reduces uncertainty and ambiguity.
- Praise helps to build Agency by allowing that person to manage any expected threats associated with the outcome.
- Approach constructive feedback with positive intent.
- Many issues with performance are the result of the failure to establish acceptance criteria for when something is complete.

Chapter 4

E IS FOR EMPATHY

"You never really know a man until you stand in his shoes and walk around in them."

—Scout, To Kill a Mockingbird

ASHAMED

I was just promoted. Many new challenges presented themselves, such as navigating difficult employee issues and learning a new software system. I was also a mom of two young children. My youngest was struggling and I needed to be with him in the late afternoons for the next two months. I was petrified about asking my new boss for this flexibility. At the time, I worked in an environment that was rigidly 8:00 am – 5:00 pm. I had seen other employees ask for even thirty minutes of flexibility and the answer was always NO. Not knowing what to do, I felt anxious because I was concerned about my son and wanted to maintain my work ethic. I did not know how to balance those two priorities. I calculated a plan to use vacation in tandem with a work shift to ensure that I wasn't a burden on other staff. The time came for the big ask. I had an ache in my stomach and felt ashamed. *Ashamed!* I felt ashamed because I was conditioned to work cultures that praised overtime and shunned vacation and sick leave.

After listening to my plan, my supervisor's face was unreadable, and I was worried that I had crossed an imaginary professional line. Then she said, "Cié, do what fits best for you. I have no doubt you will complete your job duties. Family comes first." As I absorbed those words, I could feel a huge weight begin to lift. That was not the only time she showed empathy and understanding for personal and professional situations in the two years I worked for her. It's not about what she taught me technically; it's what she taught me *empathetically* and what she taught me about myself and the balance of personal and professional responsibilities. Thanks S.B.

Now I supervise a large staff, and personal matters come up. The personal and professional lines have definitely blurred since the pandemic. Taking an empathetic approach is sometimes not easy, especially when deadlines are looming, and all your focus is on the task at hand. But it is worth the effort as it creates a climate of belonging, support, trust, and Agency.

Empathy in the context of work is the ability to relate to team members and sense what is going on in their world including the emotions being experienced.[27] It is also one of

---

27. Somogyi, Rachael L., Aaron A. Buchko, and Karen J. Buchko. "Managing With Empathy: Can You Feel What I Feel?" *Journal of Organizational Psychology* 13, no. 1/2 (2013): 32–42.

the most valued Leadership characteristics in the workplace. Research shows empathetic Leadership can help retention, motivation, and innovation.[28]

> **EMPATHY IS NEEDED NOT JUST BECAUSE IT WOULD BE NICE TO HAVE, BUT BECAUSE IT IS CRITICAL FOR PROFESSIONAL SURVIVAL**

In our current society, there is an increased need now, more than ever, for humane skills in Leadership. The pandemic showed us the need for Leaders to display self-awareness, compassion, empathy, and vulnerability.[29]

Empathy takes a back seat to the tasks and stressors of daily operations. However, it needs to be ingrained in us not because it would be nice but because it is critical for professional survival. Employees are not only dealing with the ordinary challenges of work (which can be immense) but also with societal and personal struggles.

Mass shootings, natural disasters, unpredictable economy, political drama, social justice unrest, and the list goes on. We are a significantly stressed society. According to the American Psychological Society[30], we are stressed about:

- Inflation (83%)
- Mass shootings/violent crime (75%)
- Racial climate (62%)

---

28. Brower, Tracy. "Empathy Is the Most Important Leadership Skill." *Forbes*, October 19, 2021. Accessed October 19, 2021. https://www.forbes.com/sites/tracybrower/2021/09/19/empathy-is-the-most-important-leadership-skill-according-to-research/?sh=51c40be33dc5.
29. Lawton-Misra, Nerine, and Thelma Pretorius. "Leading with Heart: Academic Leadership During the COVID-19 Crisis." *South African Journal of Psychology* 51, no. 2 (2021): 205-214.
30. American Psychological Association. "More than a Quarter of U.S. Adults Say They're So Stressed They Can't Function." October, 2022. Accessed October, 2022. https://www.apa.org/news/press/releases/2022/10/multiple-stressors-no-function.

Twenty-seven percent reported that most days they can't even function.

Gen Z adults report the highest stress levels compared to all other generations. This is the generation that is entering the workforce.

Sixty-four percent of employed adults reported that their job was a source of stress.[31]

It is also important to note that percentages of these stress levels vary based on gender, race/ethnicity, age, and other identities.

How can anyone deny that we all need empathy from others and for others, especially in professional settings? Before we proceed any further, I want to clarify that empathy is not about being too nice. I'm not advocating for wrapping your team in bubble wrap and protecting them from all external harm. Empathy is also not about throwing your boundaries out the window and getting emotionally involved.

Empathy simply means the ability to understand and share the feelings of others. It involves perceiving and relating to their thoughts, emotions, or experiences, even if we have never experienced similar things, or don't agree with their thoughts.

It's not only about positive intent with *interpersonal* communication with others, but also about positive intent with *intrapersonal* communication (the conversations

| **EMPATHY IS A CHOICE** |

---

31. American Psychological Association. "Stress in America 2020: A National Mental Health Crisis." October, 2020. Accessed October, 2020. https://www.apa.org/news/press/releases/stress/2020/report-october.

we have with ourselves). And sometimes, our internal conversations can be very judgmental about others.

Unfortunately, empathetic Leadership skills do not always come naturally. I am not calling anyone reading this an uncaring ogre. But even I, who always assumed I lead with a shiny spear of empathy, have realized, especially navigating the challenges of leading through a pandemic and leading multiple generations, how critically important empathy is and how much time leading with empathy can take. A lot of people say they lead with empathy, but, unfortunately, for many this is all too often a false assumption.

Empathy is a choice. Whether we choose to admit it or not, we sometimes pick and choose who gets our empathy. This is why self-awareness is at the core of learning to be more empathetic. It's about understanding that things may come a bit easier for you than others and vice versa. Even as I wrote this story about taking flex time for my son, I know I'm writing it from a place of privilege. Some do not have that flexibility in their jobs and careers.

Sometimes taking an empathetic approach requires us to have the Agency to evaluate a rule, policy, or current ways of doing work and ask if it still makes sense. Are we holding on to antiquated practices that are hurting our teams? Are we stuck in our concrete bunkers of how Leadership should look?

RULED BY RIGIDITY

Todd was a military veteran who worked at a university serving other military affiliated people returning to college. Todd did several tours in Iraq and was eager to share his knowledge of transitioning back to civilian life and help get the educational path started for those returning. He had been in an explosion and had recovered, but was plagued with severe migraines. Todd worked in an office environment with many cubicles, bright fluorescent lights, and a lot of noise from phones ringing to people talking. This environment exacerbated his migraine flareups.

In an effort to complete his duties and balance his health, Todd began coming into the office at 6:00 am and leaving at 2:00 pm. The quiet of the morning allowed him to work faster with the lights off and avoid the noise. He still met with students and met deadlines. However, his supervisor, Susan, didn't like that it appeared he was getting special treatment, and ordered him to return to normal working hours. He complied, but struggled and took sick leave. Todd became an 'earner and burner,' taking sick and vacation leave immediately when he earned it, thus always having a zero balance. He even took some leave without pay.

Hoping to find a compromise, Todd met with Susan and asked if he could shift his hours. He explained his health situation and assured Susan that the work would still be accomplished. However, he didn't have any medical evidence from a doctor to support his claim. Susan, firmly rooted in her fixed mindset, refused to budge. Todd resigned two weeks later. Susan didn't have the Agency to question an informal rule. She didn't want to deal with challenges and didn't want anything to 'threaten' her authority. She refused to see things from Todd's perspective nor understand where he was coming from. She closed the Door on empathy.

Empathy is *choosing* to understand. It takes time and active effort to apply empathy. Susan was only fixated on the rules. Thus, a talented, high-performing employee left. What if Susan couldn't change the rules? What else could she have done to show empathy?

Empathy holds the Door. It holds the Door for understanding. It increases Agency by letting the person know you understand where they are coming from. And by understanding where someone is coming from, suddenly, the blame or judgment becomes nonexistent.

As stated, not everyone is good at empathy, and that's okay; we are all on a messy Leadership journey. If you just read the story about Todd and are thinking, "Oh no, I'm Susan!" below are suggestions on how to approach an empathetic conversation.

- **Ask how they are**. "How are you doing"? When they say "fine," pause and ask, "How are you *really* doing"?
- **Tailor your language to the person you are speaking to**. I recall when I got my first professional job, my office used acronyms prolifically. It was like another language and made me feel woefully incompetent. Understand the knowledge level and make sure you aren't alienating someone with your 'work lingo.'
- **Validate feelings.** Just because you may not feel a high level of anxiety over an event doesn't mean someone else won't. We are all unique individuals and process events and situations very differently. You never have the right to invalidate others' emotions. To show you are open, try these phrases:
  - "That sounds challenging."

- "I understand your frustration."
- "It makes me sad/glad/mad to hear this happened."
- "Thank you for trusting me enough to share this information."
- "I would like to support you."
- "How can I support you?"
- "I'm happy to listen anytime."
- "What do you need right now?"

And remember, empathy isn't always about negative emotions. Understanding why someone is excited shows empathy too.

- "I can see why you are so excited!"
- "I understand why that is a sense of pride for you."
- "This is definitely something to be happy about."
- **Don't say anything at all; offer to listen.**

EMPATHETIC RESPECT

Empathy and respect are interconnected and complementary concepts. When we are empathetic, we open ourselves to a deeper understanding of another person's experiences and challenges. When we show respect, we recognize the inherent worth and dignity of others. This forms the basis for fair and equitable treatment. When we empathize with someone, we gain insight into their emotions, struggles, and aspirations. This understanding naturally leads to a heightened appreciation for their unique perspective and an increased inclination to treat them with respect. In return, the

> **EMPATHY AND RESPECT ARE INTERCONNECTED AND COMPLEMENTARY CONCEPTS.**

act of showing respect creates a positive environment that encourages empathy to flourish. The results can be devastating when these two important concepts are not practiced.

THE FORGOTTEN BEANS

Let's go back to the beginning – elementary school. In my fourth and fifth grade years, I was in a special program for students who were identified as gifted that met once a week. Everyone in this program was white and from financially stable families. Ten-year-old me did not realize this blatant segregation. When I started fifth grade, an additional student was added to our program, Richard. Richard was Hispanic and not from a financially stable family. I realize now how we all, consciously or unconsciously, excluded him in every way possible. The most palpable example was the Thanksgiving feast activity that we were preparing. All students were required to bring food. Richard was asked to bring two cans of beans. On the day of the feast, Richard showed up but didn't have the beans. He didn't have an answer for why; he just *forgot*.

It hurts me to write this because I can't believe I was part of such an inhumane act. We, the teacher included, berated him for not bringing the beans. He cried. He was only eleven and we broke him down over two cans of beans. Richard didn't return to the program after Thanksgiving. Looking back on this experience, I realized that Richard was from a low-income family. It never occurred to anyone in that small-town elementary school in 1988 that giving away two cans of beans, especially right before a major holiday, may not have been financially viable for his family. But there is a deeper issue. He was different. He wasn't white, wasn't 'well off,' and didn't fit the program's image. Consciously or unconsciously, we, as a collective group, drove him out because he was different. Richard, I think about you often, and I apologize.

> "We do what we know, and when we know better, we do better."
>
> – MAYA ANGELOU

How are you excluding people in your own office consciously or unconsciously? How is your office culture sending subtle messages that certain people do not fit? This can be any difference from race, gender, age, education level, or nationality.

Sadly, we sometimes make up our own definition of respect and inclusion to suit our needs.

I'll respect you by acknowledging and including you as long as you have the same opinion as I do.

or

I will show respect because we have the same values.

or

I will show empathy if you look like me and talk like me.

With Richard, there was a huge lack of empathy. There was a lack of respect for who he was and where he came from. There was a lack of empathy in understanding his point of view and lived reality.

Whether we choose to admit it or not, we are all influenced consciously or unconsciously by bias, stereotypes, and assumptions. We cancel anything we don't agree with instead of trying to seek understanding. As teams become inclusive and diverse, we shouldn't just assume our professional environments are respectful. Respect requires more of us. Intentionally considering the view through another person's eyes creates a stronger team. It isn't a passive action, but an active one. To my ten-year-old eyes, my little gifted kid class was respectful. But the respect bubble only included those that fit.

Empathy and respect go hand in hand. We should strive for it to be a standard in the workplace regardless of personal beliefs. This is especially true if we are the Leader and inescapably true if you are a Door Holder. Every person is wonderfully unique. No matter how much common ground we can find, no two people will ever have the same lived experiences. To maintain harmony in a professional relationship, it is essential for us to learn how to understand our differences and identify and be aware of our biases (conscious or unconscious).

Ask yourself these questions:

- Does every member of my team feel comfortable bringing their true self to work? How do I know?
- Can my team bring their whole selves to the office without feeling a need to hide something? How do I know?
- Is there a culture of inclusiveness and belonging, and are there mechanisms in place to find out if there isn't?

- Do I foster a climate of curiosity by approaching unknowns with an inquisitive nature to learn rather than a judgmental inclination to exclude?

It is easy to talk about what respect should look like, so let's look at some warning signs that lack of respect and lack of empathy may be present.

Boundaries are not valued. If a boundary is made known, respect it even if you personally don't understand the reason. It's not your boundary; it's their boundary. I had a coworker who did not want her birthday acknowledged publicly. Our office always put confetti and balloons on the birthday person's desk. She specifically asked for this not to occur on her birthday. On her birthday, she arrived to find her desk decorated. She broke down in something close to a panic attack. Her boundary was violated. She was feeling a lack of respect.

Dismissed feelings. A lack of respect may be present if feelings are dismissed. Is there a climate of dismissing any feelings that aren't happy? Phrases like "*You are overreacting*" or "*It's not that big of a deal,*" make someone feel as if their emotions are invalid. An empathetic approach is needed. Again, you don't have to agree with their feelings, but you can acknowledge the feelings are valid and understand why they are feeling them.

Attempts at humor. Joking around that goes too far creates a climate of disrespect. Laughing in the office is healthy unless it is at someone else's expense.

Gossip is disrespectful. Enough said.

Ignoring and excluding. If people are ignored or excluded, this could be a silent form of disrespect. Make the effort to include everyone, and if you are having activities that exclude someone, make a change. For example, are you aware of various religious holidays that may conflict with staff retreats or other teambuilding events? Do you always have happy hours that prevent some from attending? Are you conscious of food restrictions or allergies? If

> **PRACTICE HUMILITY. YOU ARE STRIVING TO BE THE DOOR HOLDER, THE GROWER, THE CULTIVATOR, NOT THE SHOWBOAT AT THE FRONT OF THE PARADE.**

you have a hybrid workforce, are you including remote employees at the same level as in-person employees?

Taking credit for others' ideas. This shows a need for more respect for the value they bring. Give credit where credit is due. Practice humility. You are striving to be the Door Holder, the grower, the cultivator, not the showboat at the front of the parade.

Microaggressions are not addressed. Any harassment or discrimination should not be tolerated. Microaggressions can be intentional or accidental comments or actions that negatively target a marginalized group or individual. These are so dangerous because the person committing them may not even realize they are doing it. But that doesn't make the impact any less harmful. Remedying microaggressions starts with awareness. Have conversations about offensive language, terminology, and actions. It may be a difficult conversation, but growth minded individuals are okay with challenging themselves. Finally, does your office have a secure outlet to report harassment, discrimination, or other forms of disrespect? Make sure that employees understand their Agency in reporting issues, where they can do this, and what the process is.

We need to own our disrespect. How often has someone brought to your attention that something you said or did was disrespectful? This is an area where it is easy for someone to dismiss feelings saying, "*It's not that big of a deal and you are overreacting.*" If you have never been called out on anything, what does that mean? If someone lets you know that what you have done or said was disrespectful, listen to them and try to understand their message, don't be defensive. An element of respect is assuming positive intent. Assuming positive intent means that you assume the intent behind their action, in this case, pointing out an act of disrespect, is not coming from a place of judgment but from a chance to inform. Assuming positive intent allows for a more empathetic approach and develops a climate of trust.

NO, YOU'RE A MOM

It was lunchtime on Friday, and Jennifer was scheduled to attend an overnight professional development retreat two days later. She was sitting in her office about to eat her ham sandwich when her Leader came to the Door. He stated, "Hey there, I have some news about the retreat."

Jennifer replied, "Yes, the Women's Professional Advancement Workshop, I'm very excited about this opportunity."

Her Leader stumbled a reply, "Yes, well, the office wasn't informed that we would have to fund your cost. We weren't expecting this expense, so I don't think you will be able to attend."

Jennifer was disappointed but understood budgetary issues. Then, her Leader stated, "...and you are a mom and have a daughter that you need to take care of, so being gone a couple of days might not be the best option."

Jennifer was in shock. At a loss for words, she simply nodded. Her Leader left.

Falling back into her office chair, she looked at her sandwich. The mix of rage, confusion, and disgust made her appetite disappear. A choice was needed: she could speak up and face whatever ramifications came from addressing this statement or stay silent and live with those outcomes.

She got up and still shaking, walked to her supervisor's office. Assuming positive intent even though her rage wanted her conversation to be much more heated, she began, "I need to ask you a question. Have I ever missed a deadline or delivered a sub-par project?"

Her Leader replied, "No, not at all; you are wonderful."

Jennifer continued, "I have an issue with the reason I'm not allowed to attend the retreat. If I can't attend because of budgetary issues, I accept that. If you have a problem with me being gone because of work performance, we need to discuss it so I can improve. My concern is that my child was brought up along with the fact that I'm a mother. My child has zero bearing on my professional performance at work and on any professional development opportunities that would enhance my job performance. I will not accept being denied an opportunity because I am a mother."

What Jennifer did by confronting an act of disrespect took Agency.

Her supervisor was receptive and thus opened an honest conversation between them both. He wasn't intending to be discriminatory, and since they both were holding the Door to empathy, they both took the time to understand. He was receptive to Jennifer's feedback about being disrespectful. Jennifer ended up going on the retreat and was eventually promoted within the office.

A respectful environment reduces stress because people feel more comfortable working with their peers, which increases productivity and collaboration. It also increases retention. Jennifer could have decided to live with disrespect, but because of the climate created within her office, she knew that if she spoke up she would be heard and listened to. Jennifer approached this tough situation in the following intentional ways:

1. She did not approach her supervisor in an accusatory way, but in a fact-finding way that opened the Door for dialogue.
2. She checked her emotions and allowed logic to lead the conversation.
3. She avoided involving other people in the office through gossip. Sometimes our first instinct is to run to a coworker and exclaim, "Can you believe what just happened?" thus making the situation worse.

It's hard not to talk about feelings when you talk about empathy. This is where many people struggle with applying empathy – setting appropriate boundaries. In conversations I've had over the years about approaching situations with empathy, I received some hesitation. People express experiencing emotional exhaustion and falling into people-pleasing tendencies. It is important to understand boundaries so that being empathetic does not reach a point that becomes detrimental to your own well-being.

HITCHHIKERS

As someone who is traveling my own road in terms of learning empathy, I realized how impactful the failure to create boundaries can be. Sometimes we blur the line between understanding where someone is coming from and just picking them up off the side of the road so we can carry them on our shoulders.

> **BEING EMPATHETIC DOESN'T MEAN YOU HAVE AN OBLIGATION TO *FIX*.**

Several years ago, I was at a national conference. It was the type of annual conference where the faces were familiar and old friends would reunite. One year, quite suddenly after dinner, a colleague asked if they could chat with me. Thinking it was just a time to catch up, I agreed, looking forward to some good conversation. It was not good. This individual was experiencing an extremely traumatic event that spanned the personal and professional. They had chosen me to share it with because they trusted me. I was caught off guard, and my desire to 'help' this person overwhelmed my rational boundary. I picked them up, internalized their feelings, and carried their burden through the conference. I allowed myself to get so emotionally hijacked that I woke up in a cold sweat and almost felt as if I was living in their situation. I didn't need to go that deep to give empathy and realized I needed to work on my own boundaries.

In discussing empathy with others, getting overinvolved is a common complaint. People assume that to be empathetic you are required to solve everyone's problems or that your time must be consumed with listening and lamenting. Many confess they become too emotionally involved to the point of creating stress in their own lives.

Being empathetic doesn't mean you have an obligation to *fix*. Everyone has a different empathetic approach, and allowing yourself to be too empathetic can result in an emotional drain. Remember these three pointers:

1. Understand the feelings of others, but don't internalize their feelings.
2. Empathy is about creating a safe space, not carrying the other person's burden.
3. You can't let yourself get emotionally hijacked. Set the boundaries that are right for you – and only you know what those boundaries are. This may take trial and error until you get it right.

"Don't set yourself on fire to keep others warm."

—PENNY REID

One way to practice empathy is to reframe the idea of empathy from a feeling to a skill. Just like conflict management skills or decision-making skills, developing empathy as a communication skill will help create the boundaries needed. Let's look at an example of breaking down empathy into a communication process.

Pretend you lead a unit that just went through a restructuring. New titles were created to genericize positions to form a career ladder. One person on your team is upset. They believed the new title was a demotion (even though there was no change in pay). Their dissatisfaction is starting to impact the quality of work and interactions with colleagues. There is no way to fix this issue, so let's look at an intentional, empathetic communication approach that holds the Door.

Use the acronym **LISTEN**

> ▶ **L**isten

Arrange a one-on-one to discuss their concerns. Sometimes people need to be heard and that's sufficient. Sometimes they need to be heard a couple of times, but it all starts with really listening. Remember how we fill the void? You, as the Leader, only know what the driving force behind the dissatisfaction is once you listen to understand. Avoid filling in the void with assumptions about why an employee is upset.

The power of listening cannot be overstated and is the most basic of skills all Leaders need. Listening holds the Door and develops Agency.

> ▶ **I**dentify the Emotions

During your discussion, attempt to understand the emotions driving this projected negativity. Perhaps this person was scared – scared of change. Emotions can hide behind other emotions.[32] Outbursts that seem like anger could be coming from a place of fear. It doesn't matter if you think this fear is irrational; it is what they are feeling, and at that time, was very rational to them.

---

32. David, Susan. "Emotional Granularity Umbrellas." October 12, 2022. Accessed October 12, 2022. https://www.susandavid.com/resource/emotional-granularity-umbrellas/.

Identify where the emotion is coming from. If it is fear, identify the root cause. Is it a past employment experience, misinformation, or comparison to another company?

- **S**elf-Awareness

If it starts to feel like a personal attack, or you find yourself falling down the rabbit hole of their emotions, take a step back. Be self-aware of how you are processing the interaction. Be self-aware of how emotionally close you are to the topic.

It's easy to misinterpret people and situations. We often bring our last conversation or the events of the day into the next interaction. We don't always know if someone is reacting to us or to something that happened earlier. It's important to have a clear head and stay intentional about what the conversation is about.

Your first reaction might be defense or annoyance. Especially if this restructuring was a benefit to open more opportunities to advance. *It's a benefit, so why is this person complaining!* Step back and manage your own emotions first. Empathy starts with self-awareness.

- **T**ake Assessment

Validate that you are correctly hearing what they are saying.

"I understand that you are feeling this way..."

"If I'm interpreting it correctly, you are feeling this because..."

The person may not even know why they are mad about the title change. Taking assessments along the way will clarify. We can be quick to assume we already know their reason when we are, in fact, woefully underinformed.

▸ **E**xpectations for Engagement

Professional settings have limits on your involvement. Set those boundaries. Set the right relationship cues. Team members need to perform, and if they don't meet expectations, the barriers to performance must be addressed. Having empathy doesn't mean you will allow this team member to continue to underperform or disrupt the rest of the team.

Explain the non-negotiables of this situation and provide support and understanding. Reiterate the overall goal, the vision, and how they fit into the picture.

▸ **N**avigate a Path Forward

In this example about a team member being upset over a title change, we can't fix anything because this person wanted their old title back. That is non-negotiable. But we can help them navigate the path forward. The path forward will be traveled much easier if the team member feels heard and valued.

Wherever you are on the empathy spectrum, small changes can yield dramatic results. Taking a moment to see things from another's perspective and appreciating the human side of work will create a healthy space.

> "To handle yourself, use your head, to handle others, use your heart."
>
> —*Eleanor Roosevelt*

THOUGHTS TO CONSIDER

- Empathy fuels people connection.
- Empathy is about recognizing that people have emotions, needs, and communicating that you recognize that.
- Empathy is balance.
- Empathy is the human part of the job.
- Empathy is allowing people to contribute all of who they are, not just part of who they are.
- Empathy is NOT sympathy.
- Empathy doesn't mean you have to agree with someone's opinions, values and beliefs.
- Empathy allows us to avoid jumping to conclusions about someone.
- Setting boundaries is important and necessary.
- Empathy starts with self-awareness.

Chapter 5

N IS FOR NEEDS

"When you say 'yes' to others make sure you are not saying 'no' to yourself."

— PAULO COELHO

A BADGE OF BURNOUT

My doctorate was completed in 3 ½ years. I'm not bragging; wait for it.

I was working full time, pursuing my doctorate, raising a family, adjunct teaching on the side at the community college across town, holding Leadership roles in state and regional professional organizations, and acting as legal guardian for an incapacitated relative. To maintain that

> **WE AREN'T ROBOTS. LACK OF SELF-CARE EVENTUALLY CAUSES US TO MALFUNCTION.**

level of unrealistic overcommitment I had to let something go. It was my health.

In a work meeting I remember a coworker calling me a robot, meaning I kept going no matter what. At the time, I was proud of that label. But we aren't robots. And lack of self-care eventually causes us to malfunction.

After working a full day, I was teaching the second class of my 5:30 p.m. to 10:00 p.m. schedule at the community college. It was Introduction to Public Speaking, the course that most students avoided until the bitter end due to fear of the obvious, speaking in public. I was determined that every student would not only pass, but also find a love for speaking. Since this was a night class, I was three times as animated to keep up the energy. It was exhausting.

The 8:00 p.m. class started. Everything was fine until I lost consciousness. I didn't fall or faint, but found myself frozen, operating in slow motion unable to react to anything around me. I was swimming in a black liquid, voices were muffled, and my mind and body were taking a break from each other. I've never blacked out mid-sentence before, almost as if my body was saying,

> *That's it, I'm done, you're done, we are just going to sit quietly for a while.*

It was terrifying.

Somehow, I managed to mumble a message to the students that class was ending early. The length of time I sat in that empty classroom was unknown, but eventually, I regained enough consciousness to drive home.

I was saying yes to everyone else but myself.

My diet was awful. I burned my candle at both ends, essentially working all the time. I never exercised, or should I say I avoided any type of exercise. Every day at 3:00 p.m. I just wanted a candy bar and a nap. My sluggishness would be remedied with a soda or coffee. My swollen feet would spill out of my shoes at the end of the day. My nights were always disrupted by acid reflux. Historically, I knew I let my health slip when I got overwhelmed, but I refused to see any of the warning signs. I needed to change my environment personally and professionally. The badge of burnout I proudly wore was slowly destroying me.

Would it surprise you to know that the top causes of burnout were unfair treatment at work, unmanageable workloads, and unreasonable time pressures?[33] Burnout isn't just about people struggling to cope with stress; it's about people struggling in workplaces where stress never stops! Some of this stress is self-imposed, like I did with myself, and other times it's the nature of the workplace environment. Workplaces are continuing to try to do more with less and continually pushing ahead despite not having the right resources or personnel. The intense focus on the numbers rather than the people creates this burnout. When we ignore the first few chapters of this book, it becomes easy to see our teams as numbers. If we fail to get to know our team and understand them as human beings, we can easily ignore their needs.

---

33. Wigert, Ben, and Sangeeta Agrawal. "Employee Burnout, Part 1: The 5 Main Causes." *Gallup*, July 12, 2018. Accessed July 12, 2018. https://www.gallup.com/workplace/237059/employee-burnout-part-main-causes.aspx.

This chapter will explore the basic needs of staff and how to create an environment that is not only healthy in the outcomes of daily work, but also healthy in the employees that perform the work. Let's start with the basics: the workday. The workday doesn't equate to a person's entire day. Sometimes deadlines and projects make us forget that. To understand the needs of your staff and avoid burnout, let's start with understanding the workday beyond the logistics of hours and duties.

INCONVENIENT SICK LEAVE

Justine worked at the same company for ten years. As the lead support staff, she would always work fifty-to-sixty-hour weeks. She was a loyal employee even though the salary was low, which forced her to take a second job on nights and weekends to make finances work.

Justine needed surgery. It was minor and just an overnight procedure, but she had been putting it off. However, working through her pain was no longer an option. She informed her supervisor that she would be out for two days, taking some of the hundreds of hours of unused sick leave that she had accumulated. Being a detailed person, she made sure everything was in order before she left so she could focus on recovery.

The morning of the operation, she was sitting in the operating waiting room. She received a text message. She paused, wanting to ignore it, but habit kicked in and she reviewed the message. It was from her supervisor, who wanted her to look over some reports. A bit annoyed, she replied, reminding him that she was out for surgery for the next two days.

He responded, "Well, what time are you out of surgery today? Can you look over the reports now while you are just waiting or after your procedure and let me know before 5:00?"

You may not be surprised to find out that Justine is no longer in that position. She quit and found a position that valued her needs as a **human being** and the value of sick leave.

Justine's supervisor was creating an unhealthy environment that fostered burnout. If you are concerned that you might be creating a burnout conducive environment, there are signs to be aware of.

Watch your communication. When do you communicate with staff, and what are their expectations about communicating with you? I used to send emails after hours so I would remember my thoughts. I noticed my staff would reply and try to solve the request immediately, even late at night. I stopped. Be a healthy example of a balanced work/home life. Yes, issues that require after hours communication will come up, but make it the exception and not the rule. Employees need that balance and permission to disconnect.

Plan for vacations. When people are going to be out of the office for a length of time, encourage them to have a point person to take care of their duties. This allows for cross-training and confidence building. This also allows that vacationer to relax. Respect vacation or sick leave as that individual's personal time, and they should not be contacted for tasks or information that is easily shared or provided by another until they return. We all need vacations, not only physically being in another location, but mentally as well. If we are worried that our office is in turmoil because we took a vacation, relaxation will never occur.

Practice transparency. The workday may need to shift to meet certain demands. Be transparent about this and how it will affect schedules. Respect that people have arrangements to be made for children, pets, elderly parents, or others in their care. They may come from a household that shares a car or other duties that will have to be rearranged. Yes, events and tasks will require us to work outside of the normal hours, but being transparent with advanced notice will lessen stress and anxiety. People need time to manage unexpected schedule disruptions.

Respect time. If you schedule a meeting, start and end it on time. If you have back-to-back meetings, put in a ten-minute buffer so you can be on time. If you ask everyone to arrive for an event at 8:00 a.m., you need to arrive at 7:45 a.m., not 8:15. If you have asked someone to come in early, let them leave early, too. Allow for breaks; don't question why someone was away from their desk. Respecting people's time is respecting their needs.

At the start of the pandemic, a coworker in another department shared with me that she felt so much pressure to be 'present' while working remotely that she took her computer with her to the bathroom. Do you expect your team to work from the bathroom? Better question, do *they* think you expect them to work from the bathroom?

Analyze the workloads. Are staff required to be superhuman? Is it feasible to com-

> **YOUR PROCRASTINATION IS NOT YOUR TEAM'S PRIORITY.**

plete what is being asked of them in the hours they have? Evaluate if the deliverables you are asking for are achievable in the amount of time expected. Analyze your own workload. Are you constantly giving last-minute tasks to your team because you run out of time to do them? Your procrastination is not your team's priority.

Speaking of time management, offer time management training. Sometimes, poor time management is the culprit in an unbalanced workload. Use this as a teachable moment. Also, respect how people work; they may work at a different pace but still get the job done.

Watch for burnout signs. Finally, don't let your staff become burnt pieces of toast. Someone who is struggling will be tired, stressed, distant, and become more likely to make mistakes. If you have built a one-on-one connection, you will be able to spot burnout a lot easier. You must look for the signs. And the signs are there if we choose not to ignore them.

I had the pleasure of hearing Michael Ciannilli, a Program Manager from NASA, deliver a presenta-

> **IN OUR DESIRE FOR PROGRESS WE CAN BECOME BLIND TO REAL ISSUES THAT NEED ATTENTION.**

tion about lessons learned from the Apollo, Challenger, and Columbia disasters. The presentation outlined some of the warning signs on the ground that were missed. Alone, they may have been seen as insignificant, however, added together revealed a much greater issue. He stated, "the 'system' was talking, but no one was listening." He further discussed that in a team there are links in the chain that lead to a certain outcome. If one of those links is broken, missing, or not working, the outcome can be dramatically affected.[34]

How do you know if there is a broken link? He explained, it's not just about listening to your team; it's about hearing them. We are geared to respond when we listen, always waiting for our turn to talk and thinking about how we are going to reply. To identify what the system is saying, we must listen to what is not being said. We must put aside our biases and notions of how we want it to be and see the reality. In our desire for progress, we can become blind to real issues that need attention. There is strength and wisdom in the Agency to say 'no go.' To do this we must open the Door and approach listening with fresh ears every time, even if the person speaking up was wrong in the past.

The 'system' is talking to us, but can we cut through the noise enough to listen? Your team is revealing issues. Alone, they may seem insignificant, but added together could reveal a major issue. Are you hearing them? Do you have an environment in which discussing needs is valued? Do you have a psychologically safe environment?

PSYCHOLOGICAL SAFETY

Given all the stressors of life that people must deal with day to day, it is hard to argue that people desperately need a sense of safety in their professional lives now more than ever. Psychological safety is a belief that one will not be punished or humiliated for speaking up with ideas, questions, con-

---

34. Ciannilli, Michael. "Communication Lessons from the Columbia Tragedy." Presentation at the National Speakers Association Conference, Nashville, TN, 2022.

cerns, or mistakes.[35] Feeling safe in your professional environment means the confidence to show up to work as your true self, where you know you will be respected and valued. Psychological safety is acknowledgment, the ability to grow with support and encouragement, and knowing that you have an empathetic environment in which to operate where your basic needs will be met. A psychologically safe environment holds the Door and allows Agency to increase.

A critical part of a Leader's role is promoting psychological safety so people can openly discuss ideas and concerns without fear.[36] This is sometimes a hard concept to convey as the elements of a psychologically safe environment are dynamic. You can't just slap a label on the office door that proclaims the area SAFE. It involves a constant feedback loop, observation, and making sure that everyone feels safe, not just some.

The restraints of an environment that is not psychologically safe are detrimental to the employees, Leaders, and the whole organization. It may not be immediately noticeable, and that is why, as the Leader, it is your job to be aware. Practice intentional communication with positive intent, work to establish professional growth in your employees, and hold the Door empathetically, understanding unique needs of your team. As the Leader and the Door Holder, you must ac-

---

35. Edmondson, Amy C. *The Fearless Organization: Creating Psychological Safety in the Workplace for Learning, Innovation, and Growth.* Hoboken, NJ: John Wiley & Sons, 2019.
36. D'Auria, Gianpiero, and Aaron De Smet. "Leadership in a Crisis: Responding to the Coronavirus Outbreak and Future Challenges." March 16, 2020. Accessed March 16, 2020. https://www.mckinsey.com/capabilities/people-and-organizational-performance/our-insights/leadership-in-a-crisis-responding-to-the-coronavirus-outbreak-and-future-challenges#/.

knowledge your role in creating a psychologically safe ecosystem.

I was at lunch with a coworker. She is someone I've known for years and has recently started excelling in her job, receiving two internal promotions in the last two years. She has been with the same office for eight years but had stagnant growth until recently. This sudden propulsion forward was intriguing. The only thing that changed was her office Leadership.

Reflecting on her success, I asked, "What happened to you? It's like you are a different person. You are so confident?"

She replied, "The Leadership is different now. I didn't want to be a Leader under the old Leader."

We continued our conversation, and I asked why she didn't want to be a Leader under the old Leader. She responded with the following description of a psychologically **un**safe environment:

- Mistakes were made public and ridiculed.
- New ideas were discouraged.
- Everyone was scared to try anything new for fear of failure.
- The Leadership operated under the motivator of fear instead of empowerment.
- Gossip was rampant and the Leader participated.
- The Leader had favorites, and there were cliques.
- Promises were made but never kept.
- There was an absence of trust.
- Underperformers were valued only if they held the same views as Leadership.

This is an environment that destroys creativity, innovation, and collaboration. It is tainted soil where nothing can flourish. There is no Agency growing in this wasteland of toxicity.

In a psychologically **un**safe environment, you can hold the Door, but no one will feel safe enough to walk through it. My colleague is the same person with the same skills, but she withered under one Leader and flourished under another. Being aware of the environment that your team works in is critical to building Agency and holding the Door.

These are signs that your workplace environment may have low psychological safety.
- Employees don't ask questions, ever.
- When mistakes are made, blaming others is the first reaction instead of owning the mistake.
- Hot topic issues are simply avoided.
- The phrase "that's not my job" or "that's above my paygrade" is often used. *These are fixed mindset comments.*
- There is a failure to manage agreement; meaning everyone agrees with anything that is said because there is a fear of rocking the boat, or they just want to get it done regardless of the quality of the delivery.
- People will agree with a bad decision because that is less of a risk than speaking up.
- Bullying, intimidation, bias, or other forms of discrimination are present.

It is important to note that psychological safety is not a one-size-fits-all. Those with social privileges may be experiencing psychological safety when others are not. Diversity in teams creates better outcomes due to the richness of varied contribution of ideas. However, just because you have a diverse team doesn't mean everyone has the same level of psychological safety. It's important to understand that we all are an amalgamation of different identities. Individuals have multiple social realities or identities that are experienced at the same time.[37] This is why creating a psychologically safe environment takes understanding ALL who occupy it.

Changing an unsafe environment into a safe one can take time, especially to start gaining the trust of the employees. If you see similarities in your office with some of the unsafe characteristics, act now. Opening the Door to a psychologically safe environment can start with something as simple as a conversation where you listen with positive intent to honest feedback. However, creating a psychologically safe environment does not simply mean avoiding all negatives and saying, 'Everything is fine'. This results in toxic positivity.

EVERYTHING IS FINE! IGNORE THE FIRE

A contributor to an unsafe psychological environment is something known as toxic workplace positivity. This is the enforcement of the need for everything to be fine, or at least appear fine, overriding any emotions or issues. This can alienate people and cause stress. Psychological safety is not

> **PSYCHOLOGICAL SAFETY IS NOT ABOUT YOUR TEAM ALWAYS BEING HAPPY; IT'S THE FREEDOM TO HAVE DIALOGUE WHEN THINGS ARE NOT HAPPY.**

---

37. Dill, Bonnie Thornton, Angela E. McLaughlin, and Angela D. Nieves. "Future Directions of Feminist Research: Intersectionality." In *Handbook of Feminist Research*, edited by Sharlene Nagy Hesse-Biber, 629–637. Thousand Oaks, CA: SAGE Publications, 2007.

about your team always being happy; it's the freedom to have dialogue when things are not happy. Toxic positivity is simply a masked, unsafe environment. For example, when Jennifer spoke up about the statement from her leader about her being a mother, it was because the environment was one in which she felt she could speak up. Just because an environment is safe, doesn't mean uncomfortable conversations will never happen. It means that when these conversations need to happen, people feel safe and empowered to have them. It is about the ability to talk about the good and the bad with an approach of positive intent and empathy in hopes of an agreeable outcome. If no one is coming to you with any issues ever, and you believe that everything is fine, you may be dwelling in toxic positivity.

Another term that can be used in an 'everything is fine' situation is seduction of the Leader, which has several interpretations.[38] First, it means the unconscious seducing of the leader into believing there are no issues. Negative information, conflicts, scarcities, cases of burnout, and other unpleasantries, are not shared with the leader but rather hidden away. This generally occurs with a Leader at a higher level.

The second interpretation is that the team will never contradict the Leader's style of leadership. If the style is not working or even counterproductive, the team will stay silent and work extra to fix the damage the Leader has created. The Leader in this situation has a personality that is not open to suggestions or opinions, and since it all appears to be working, they believe they are leading effectively.

---

38. Sanaghan, Patrick. "The Seduction of the Leader: The Superintendent's Dilemma." *American Association of School Administrators*, July 2011.

The third interpretation of the seduction of the Leader is the phenomenon of while the team is seducing the Leader, they are seducing themselves. In this "if you build it, they will come" scenario, pretending everything is fine will magically make it so. This creates a twilight zone of functioning where no Doors are being held and Agency has no chance to develop.

For several years, when I facilitated a leadership development program, we deviated from the traditional method of reading a nonfiction leadership book to reading a work of fiction. The book *Watership Down* by Richard Adams is a fictional story about rabbits and their search for a new home after their warren was destroyed.[39] This tale about talking rabbits proved to serve as a level playing field for the cohort, and there were many lessons based on the analysis of Leadership effectiveness and ineffectiveness displayed by characters in the book. There were good rabbit Leaders and bad rabbit Leaders, and many other translatable storylines that are relevant to professional contexts.

Part of the book that I always found extremely unsettling (because it mirrored professional situations too closely) was when the small troupe of traveling rabbits came upon what seemed like an absolute paradise. The rabbits in this utopian warren were healthy and strong, food was always abundant, and there was an absence of predators. The traveling rabbits were welcomed and invited to stay. However, the traveling rabbits noticed an unsettling pattern. Inhabitants of this utopia would suddenly disappear. When the traveling rabbits would inquire about the missing resident, the others acted

---

39. Adams, Richard. *Watership Down*. New York: Scribner, 1972.

as if nothing was out of the ordinary, even pretending that rabbit never existed. Fiver, the smallest of the traveling rabbits, tried to explain something was wrong, but he was dismissed with that familiar phrase, "Everything is fine; you are overreacting." Actually, something was incredibly wrong with this warren.

The reason for the abundance of food and zero threat of predators was the fact that a farmer was harvesting rabbits for food. He would feed and protect them so he could eat them. Snares were strategically set up so when an unsuspecting rabbit would get caught, they were swiftly yanked away and thus disappeared to the farmer's dinner table. The utopian rabbits had seduced themselves to ignore this negative event and proceed as if everything was *fine*.

What snares are being ignored in your professional environment? What has gone to the dinner table that you refuse to discuss? What issues are you shutting down with toxic positivity or seduction of the leader? Are you a leader who is being seduced?

> "Optimism doesn't mean that you are blind to the reality of the situation. It means that you remain motivated to seek a solution to whatever problems arise."
>
> — *The Dalai Lama*

I DON'T KNOW, AND THAT'S OKAY

> **A PSYCHOLOGICALLY SAFE ENVIRONMENT ALLOWS SPACE FOR HONESTY.**

We agree that uncertainty makes us uncomfortable and therefore we are always looking to reduce it. We are all faced with situations in which we don't know the answer. Being stuck in that dark abyss of *I don't know* can be intimidating, frustrating, and create feelings of inadequacy. Sometimes we create a climate of toxic positivity because we feel an answer must be provided to make everyone feel *fine*. There are some lessons to be learned in embracing and accepting that sometimes "I don't know" is the answer, and it can be given with confidence instead of guilt or fear when it is used to further a conversation. A psychologically safe environment allows space for honesty.

A small caveat: there is a difference between not knowing something because the information is unavailable or ever-changing and not knowing something because you haven't been properly trained or followed through with individual learning. Refer to Chapter 3 about growth when there is a lack of knowledge about a skill or task that requires specific direction and development of a growth mindset. For those other ambiguous times, there are different ways to say, "I don't know."

- ▸ I don't have enough information to answer your question currently, but this is what I do know.
- ▸ That is a developing situation, and more research is needed before I can give an accurate answer. Let's brainstorm possible research that can lead us to more clarity.

- That is a very valid question and one that I'm seeking an answer to as well. Have you investigated this question? What knowledge do you have?
- Let's review what we do know.
- Based on the facts that we have in front of us, we can determine the following is true.
- Based on the knowledge I have right now (or based on my current understanding), I can confirm the following. Now let's list the items that need further clarification.

These statements open a Door for dialogue and discovery. By creating an environment of discovery and welcoming questions and inquiry, you create a safe space for staff to ask the questions needed to bring clarity to unknown situations. Here are other ways to reduce ambiguity and uncertainty to build psychological safety.

Explore stress. As stress levels increase, we lose our ability to think clearly so we can rationally approach a situation. It is also important to note that we all handle stress differently and can become stressed by different triggers. Changes in staff, resources, and even location of work (home vs. office) create this stress. Add global issues such as pandemics, natural disasters, civil unrest, politics, and everyday personal struggles, and you have a boiling pot of anxiety. Exploring these with staff will make them visible and hopefully minimize conclusion jumping.

Explain allocation of limited resources. If resources are cut, does your team know how to shift focus and priorities? Do not take for granted that they do. Have a clear conversation about what is available right now and how, as a team, everyone will use what they must to move forward. Sometimes people need to understand it is ok to do less with less.

Discuss role ambiguity or role incompatibility. This is about creating a safe environment where people feel free to share their 'I don't knows.' Even changing environments (remote to home) can feel like a job duty shift. Have these open conversations, praise the work and effort that has been displayed, and make sure everyone is on the same page about their daily tasks.

> **SOMETIMES A PSYCHOLOGICALLY UNSAFE ENVIRONMENT IS CREATED BY OTHERS ON THE TEAM.**

Missing (wrong) information. Squash rumors as soon as they surface. Call it by its name, "That is a rumor that does not have evidence to prove it is a fact. Please do not spread rumors." Sometimes a psychologically unsafe environment is created by others on the team.

Manage emotions. Feelings are real and it is alright to feel them. Create a space for sharing and listening to staff. You do not have to agree with their feelings but having empathy will help you understand where these feelings originate from.

THOUGHTS TO CONSIDER

- Burnout is an outcome of unfair treatment at work, unmanageable workloads, and unreasonable time pressures.
- Your procrastination is not your employee's priority.
- The system is talking, are you listening?
- People need a sense of safety in their professional lives.
- Toxic positivity is harmful.
- It's ok to not have an answer for everything.

> "Leadership must first and foremost meet the needs of others."
>
> — *Robert Greenleaf*

Chapter 6

C IS FOR CONFIDENCE

"You are perfectly cast in your life. I can't imagine anyone but you in the role. Go play."

– LIN-MANUEL MIRANDA

SALAD FORK

I was three years into an entry-level staff position at a large public university. Following my time as a middle and high school teacher, this position was my first office job. For efficiency, I started working at the same university where I was pursuing my master's degree. What started out as a placeholder position was slowly blossoming into something I was passionate about.

As a young professional, I made mistakes along the way, including breaking the shredder and having an Associate Dean reduce me to tears (unrelated incidents). However, I was a key contributor to several new projects and initiatives, received good performance reviews, and began asking for added responsibility.

The university implemented a Leadership development program with the goal of identifying potential executive level talent. It was a yearlong program sponsored by the President. Candidates for this competitive program were nominated. I didn't even know I was nominated until I received a letter congratulating me on being accepted into the program.

At the first program session, I was sitting at one of the round tables making small talk. I immediately recognized names and was impressed with the caliber of people I would get to spend the next year with. Then, official introductions begin. Suddenly, I got that sinking feeling. A clammy sweat began to form, and my throat felt constricted. All the other participants were mid-manager and up titles, had been at the university five to fifteen years longer than I, and had more advanced degrees. There was Dr. So and So, Executive Director... and I'm just Cié. All my perceived inadequacies came bubbling up to the surface.

> *How can I have intelligent conversations?*
>
> *What happens when they find out who I am?*
>
> *I have to eat a fancy catered lunch with these people every month! Which fork is the salad fork?*

My heart was racing as my turn to introduce myself came nearer. I was certain when I said I was entry-level without an advanced degree and had only been here three years, they would say, "Whoa, how did you get in here? You need to leave. Someone made a mistake. You don't belong here."

I felt less than.

I felt like an imposter.

I felt these thought distortions for at least the first six months of the program. I was too much *this* and not enough *that*.

I felt I was being judged at every turn, even to the level of table etiquette mastery! But guess what? I was never asked to leave.

Raise your hand if at some point in your career you feared someone was going to knock on your office door and say, "We found out you don't know what you are doing, pack up, let's go. You don't belong here."

Some of you are thinking that right now.

Confidence in yourself is so important and is a critical attribute in a Leadership role.[40] It takes confidence to hold the Door and confidence to walk through it. If you feel that you are the only one who struggles with confidence, let me assure you, you are not alone. We think we are the only ones; we never are.

This chapter explores triggers of self-doubt and confidence building techniques that you can analyze to improve yourself and others. We will look at several causes of lack of confidence as well as ways to build it. We will also call out that destructive voice inside your head that tells you evil little lies about being *less than*. This will help you as the Door Holder build confidence within your own Leadership and allow you to understand how to build it in others.

Personally, one of the most rewarding accomplishments of my career is seeing people grow. It's not the initiatives I've

---

40. Kouzes and Posner, "Leadership Challenge"

implemented or the reports I have written. It's the holding of the Door for new Leaders to flourish. It's building confidence in someone else.

MUZZLE THE NOISE

What does that negative voice inside your head sound like? Is it the high pitch squeak of an annoying small dog, or is it a deep snarling growl that forces you to accept your inadequacies?

A common way to discuss confidence issues is the term imposter syndrome, which has been around since the 1970's.[41] Imposter syndrome is an inability to believe that one's success is deserved or legitimate.[42] You are somehow faking it and it will eventually be revealed that you are an imposter. Believing this can impede growth and progress. Viewing ourselves through this lens causes us to overthink and second-guess.

I want to add a bit of caution about throwing around the term imposter syndrome. It can be used too loosely. Just because you feel unsure about something doesn't mean you are an imposter. And every time you enter a new situation, using the term should not be a default. I also argue that sometimes we need to build skills. Just because you don't have the skills now doesn't mean you are an imposter.

It is also important to note that imposter syndrome looks different for different people. As a female, I may feel a differ-

---

41. Clance, Pauline R., and Suzanne A. Imes. "The Impostor Phenomenon in High Achieving Women: Dynamics and Therapeutic Intervention." *Psychotherapy: Theory, Research & Practice* 15, no. 3 (1978): 241–247.
42. Sakulku, Jaruwan, and James Alexander. "The Imposter Phenomenon." *International Journal of Behavioral Sciences* 6, no. 1 (2011): 75–97.

ent type of imposterism than my male colleague. We have all been exposed to discrimination, biases, or other systemic influences, and the amount of exposure and type of exposure differ from person to person. The development of Leadership confidence is personal, and we are all coming from different standpoints. Self-doubt can manifest from many different places because we all have unique lived experiences. Your colleague may have confidence in something you have extremely low confidence in. It is critical to understand these nuances. However, for the sake of covering self-doubt the following discussion will be in a generic context.

Kris Kelso, a colleague, leadership coach, and entrepreneur, wrote a book on imposter syndrome.[43] In visiting with him, he told me that he still deals with self-doubt when discussing the content of his book. So, he has imposter syndrome about being the author of the book he researched and wrote on imposter syndrome. My conversation with him was validating, as I too, have had self-doubt writing this book.

> AS LEADERS WE DO NOT HAVE TO BE PERFECT, AND OWNING SOME OF THAT IMPERFECTION, THAT VULNERABILITY, MAKES US HUMAN AND THUS MORE ABLE TO CONNECT.

Calling this self-doubt out and learning to reframe it for yourself and others is critical in becoming the Door Holder and increasing Agency. A few years ago, in a workshop I was presenting on this topic, I talked about how I had to battle self-doubt in creating the very training I was giving about overcoming self-doubt. I was open, honest, and authentic.

---

43. Kelso, Kris. *Overcoming the Imposter: Silence Your Inner Critic and Lead with Confidence.* Nashville, TN: Dexterity, 2021.

In reading the surveys, several people noted that they found it astonishing that I would be doubtful as I came across as confident. They also noted the validation that I struggled was helpful to them in understanding their own struggles. As Leaders we do not have to be perfect, and owning some of that imperfection, that vulnerability, makes us human and thus more able to connect.

It's easy to fill in the meaning of a situation. We can create the false narrative that we are the only ones struggling or we are the only ones who don't have it all figured out. That's simply not the case. A lot of our cognitive distress is over things that don't even exist.

Where does lack of self-confidence come from? Lack of self-confidence grows in different places for different people. It could be carried from childhood, or a constant message told by a person in authority.

> **UNDERSTANDING WHAT CAN TRIGGER SELF-DOUBT CAN HELP YOU HOLD THE DOOR FOR CONFIDENCE BUILDING.**

It could be from systemic forces of power that push stereotypical messages on us to the point we believe them. Self-doubt can be ignited by something new: a new Leadership role, new project, or new technology. It may seem we are always living with confidence issues, but if we take a step back and analyze when they flare up, we can see a pattern and prepare better for them. Regardless of where these feelings originate or when they are triggered in the professional world, the reality is that everyone struggles in this area at some point. Some struggle with it to the point of crippling growth and progression professionally. Self-reflection on where your confidence issues pop up the most can help you mitigate. Understanding what can trigger self-doubt can help you hold the Door for confidence building.

The frustrating and encouraging thing about confidence is that to have or not have it is largely controlled by our thoughts. My confidence in my running ability was controlled by my false perception of a lack of athletic stamina which was just a piece of floor on my face. My confidence in my ability to be engaged in professional Leadership development was controlled by my negative self-talk of not having the right title or degree.

Negative self-talk is the inner dialogue that is destructive in nature about our perceived flaws or weaknesses. Allow me to reiterate *perceived* flaws or weaknesses. It is an outside influence that we have internalized.

If negative self-talk is an **Outside** influence that we have **Internalized**, can you trace the outside influence? Ask yourself these questions:

1. Where do you think these messages come from?
2. Do you know how long you have had them?
3. How do you feel these negative thoughts are impacting your professional life?
4. What emotions result from these negative thoughts?

Asking yourself these questions and reflecting on them could be uncomfortable, but it is necessary to get in the mud and wrestle with these thoughts. These thoughts are called cognitive distortions and can cause us to perceive reality inaccu-

> **THESE THOUGHTS ARE CALLED COGNITIVE DISTORTIONS AND CAN CAUSE US TO PERCEIVE REALITY INACCURATELY.**

rately.[44] Our thoughts influence whether we have a good day or a bad day, take something personal, or simply let it roll off our backs. Our mind is very powerful, and it is often the culprit that slams the Door.

Cognitive Distortions can cause us to:
1. Believe something is true when it isn't.
2. Believe something is NOT true when it is.
3. Increase negative feelings and emotions.
4. Communicate ineffectively or cryptically.
5. Stunt professional growth.
6. Impact team performance.

Below are some examples of the most common cognitive distortions, and examples of how they play out in professional contexts.[45]

---

44 Burns, David D., and Melvin D. Burns. *Feeling Good: The New Mood Therapy*. New York: Signet Books, 1980.
45. Grohol, John M. "15 Common Cognitive Distortions." *PsychCentral*, May 17, 2016. Accessed May 17, 2016. https://psychcentral.com/lib/cognitive-distortions-negative-thinking.

Definition	Example
Mind Reading - Assuming you know what another is thinking based on little to no evidence.	*The new boss didn't say hi to me this morning in the breakroom. She must think I'm not very important in this office.*
Overgeneralization – Predictions are made about the future based on little evidence or facts.	*The boss scheduled a meeting at 4 p.m. on Friday. I'm getting fired.*
Magnification – Exaggerating our faults or mistakes.	*I forgot to schedule the Monday morning meeting. I'm not organized at all and will be written up.*
Minimization – Undervaluing our strengths and positive qualities.	*I received positive comments after the report but it was still a mess, and I don't think anyone understood my data.*
Emotional Reasoning - We avoid what makes us uncomfortable; use feelings and emotions to drive us.	*I'm so anxious about this presentation I think I will ask someone else to give it for me.*
Personalization – Taking responsibility for things outside your control.	*I feel so bad that everyone hated the lunch that was catered at today's event.*
Labeling – Create a broad label for yourself.	*The team didn't like my activity at the retreat. I am not a teambuilder.*
Should Statements – Scrutinize a conversation, or ourselves.	*I SHOULD be more likeable. I SHOULD have researched this more. I SHOULD have asked more questions in the meeting.*

Adapted from Grohol

It's important to understand how these distortions can influence your behavior. Listening to your staff can help identify when some of these thought distortions are present. Openly talking about self-doubt in a safe space increases motivation, connection, and leads to a more psychologically safe environment. It increases empathy to know that someone else knows what it feels like to not have it all figured out.

It's one thing to muzzle these intrusive thoughts, but to truly grow you need to change their behavior.

OBEDIENCE TRAINING

If we have control of anything in our lives, we have control over how we speak to ourselves. We have the power to change the meaning of these internal thoughts. Reframing simply means having the Agency to identify self-doubt or negative internal thoughts (cognitive distortions) and reframing them in a growth-minded way. Instead of just keeping those thoughts muzzled, learn how to re-train them for good. By reframing, you become in charge instead of your negative dialogue barking the orders. Many deficit-driven internal thoughts come from a place that has no evidence to prove its accuracy. Below is a path for navigating someone (or yourself) through negative distortions.

First, start with identifying the internal thought, the triggers, and the emotions associated with it. A good tool in reframing is to understand how this is impacting your professional life. By stepping back, you may be able to see there are more ramifications than previously realized. For example, looking at the chart, if you are telling yourself that you are not an effective presenter, identify when this is triggered for you.

Is it when you receive impromptu requests and you do not have time to prepare? Or when the audience is a certain size? What emotions are you filled with? Fear? Anxiety?

Second, find the evidence. Is there proof that validates this negative self-talk around the claim that you are not an effective presenter? If there is evidence that your presentation skills could improve, identify what those are and set an action plan to improve them. This puts you on the road to growth rather than living in the fixed cage of "I'm not an effective presenter."

What's the Internal Thought?	What triggers the thought? What are the emotions?	What's the impact on my professional life?
I am not an effective presenter.	Impromptu requests Diverse audience Audience size Fear, anxiety, incompetence	Avoid presentations Weakens networking Other work suffers due to obsessing over this topic
Where is the evidence for this thought?	**What action can I take to reframe this thought?**	**The NEW Internal Thought!**
Where is the evidence that I am a terrible presenter? Have I received feedback? From the audience, peers, or supervisor? Am I meeting my other work deliverables? What am I telling myself that could be false? What is a positive aspect of presenting?	Practice presentations (start by hosting small meetings) Be prepared with better notes, and practice Ask for honest feedback What can I use as a growth opportunity? How can I reframe how I look at presenting?	*I can be a more effective presenter by:* Building confidence with smaller audiences to reduce fear Getting feedback and taking it as a growth opportunity to increase belief in ability Utilizing strengths Templates for impromptu requests to reduce anxiety

By having a one-on-one connection with your staff and having set the stage for a growth mindset, you can identify negative internal dialogue and help them navigate a path toward reframing.

Starting conversations about thought distortions can be tricky. Below are some phrases to help you get started.

"I notice that when we discuss this topic, you reference a mistake you made in the past. Is there concern on your part about your ability to complete that task? I welcome any feedback so I can understand how to support you."

"Our one-on-ones have been canceled the last three times. Does this time slot conflict? Would you prefer to schedule a different reoccurring meeting? I have several agenda items that I would like to discuss."

"I would like to review my (or your) performance over the past six months and make sure we are on the same page with expectations."

"I really appreciate and value your expertise on this subject. I would like to discuss ideas I have and get your input moving forward."

"Your presentations are very good. Can we meet for coffee? I'd like to gather some pointers to build my skills in that area."

"I'd like to discuss the project that you are leading. It is behind based on the timeline created. Let's discuss it, and I'm happy to provide more clarification if needed."

"I'd like ten minutes of your time to clarify the email that was sent."

"I would like to discuss my personal Leadership style and learn yours as well. I know styles are different, so I'd like to have a conversation so we can be as efficient and collaborative as possible."

"We have worked together for many years, and I value you as a colleague. I'd like to discuss your Leadership growth potential and get some feedback."

"I understand you have joined our team from another office and recognize the expectations may have been very different. Let's meet to discuss any concerns, questions, and expectations you have."

CONFIDENCE VAMPIRES

In many of the workshops or trainings that I have done with professionals, a consistent source of confidence issues is a past toxic work environment or supervisor. These confidence vampires have literally drained the self-assurance out of staff. Many of these environments were not psychologically safe and, as a result, people are struggling in the fallout. This section will break down the ramifications of a toxic work environment and provide steps for recovery.

In speaking with employees who are recovering from a negative past working environment, it was not one major event that made the environment dysfunctional, but a collection of small events that mounted over time.

For example, you could have a grumpy boss who isn't overly polite or congenial. Maybe he or she got very mad and slammed fists against the table and yelled in a meeting. That's one event, but the wearing down comes not from that one bite, but all the others that don't heal before the next one comes. These could include:
- Small snaps of unpredictable anger that cause people to live in fear. You never know when your boss will wel-

come you into the office or when they will scream at you to leave.
- Whispers, rumors, or gossip behind your back.
- Another project, program, or report that is flawless that you were asked to work overtime on, but there is no recognition.
- Constant lack of acknowledgment for your efforts.
- A continuous *pants on fire* environment where everything is a high priority and planning is deficient.
- Constant expectations to clear up other's mistakes and being ridiculed if you do not.
- Microaggressions.

One confidence vampire bite is bad, but 1000 bites over time is much worse; you are not completely healed from the last one when another one comes along. We hold onto these past events because emotions, beliefs, and sensations from trauma or distress are encoded in memory. All these little bites are embedded in our memory, and since we are still in a professional environment where these occurred, the triggers are still there.

Signs that a team continue to be haunted by these vampires may not be easily recognizable, and the fact they are still being affected is not their fault. We are hardwired to do it. Biologically we grew to be adaptive to dangers in the environment, and if we forget a dangerous event, we might repeat it. If I forgot that the lion almost ate me, he might really get me next time. We may feel if we forget or move on from how we were treated it will happen again.

We interpret things based on our previous scripts – our past experiences. Sometimes it is hard to separate, we are in a new play (new professional context) but are still reading from the old script (our old past toxic professional context). People can be in a good work environment now, but still be waiting for the other shoe to drop. Recall the team members who were uncomfortable with praise because it had always come with bad news? They came from toxic past environments.

It's time to put a stake through the heart of confidence vampires, you have the power, you have the Agency to do so. You may not be able to erase the past, but you can ensure that you hold the Door and build confidence for the future. The preceding chapters lead you through creating interactions that feed into confidence building. Use that to hold the Door. You may not realize how impactful that can be, because the bite of a confidence vampire can last an extremely long time.

A TALE OF TWO LEADERS

When I was a sophomore in high school, my friend and I spontaneously decided to sign up for one of the new spring sports that was introduced to our tiny, small town high school. Our choices were golf or tennis. We chose golf based on the critical distinction that it would have less running than tennis. I had never held a golf club in my life. Coach Bradford was a young, new coach who accepted our naivete and probably knew we picked golf because we thought it was easy.

He balanced teaching actual skill with motivating praise for effort even when I only hit the ball a couple of feet. He would spend time trying to find balls that had been hit into the rough so I wouldn't have to take a penalty or just give me another ball to hit when it was clear mine was hopelessly lost. As a golf team, we competed in tournaments in other small rural towns; sometimes on golf courses that looked more like pastureland, even with a few cows. I don't think we ever won, but he was always proud of our effort. I never saw him mad or frustrated. He took us for who we were, he got to know us and valued our strengths and weaknesses. Because of this, we were a great team.

At the time, I didn't realize what was happening. Coach Bradford was growing my confidence, building my Agency, and holding the Door.

I still play golf, and when I prepare to swing the club, I still remember the techniques he taught me so many years ago. But here's the kicker: I'm not really that good at golf but I'm still confident. I still swing and miss the ball, hit into the sand trap, and rarely par a hole. But I am confident and always willing to try. I have Agency that I can deal with whatever outcomes may unfold out on the fairway.

Writing this, I don't think I can articulate what he did to make me confident in golf. It was an amalgamation of patience and kindness, meeting me where I was, building my skills, and expecting me to improve. It was his acknowledgment, commitment to my growth, empathy, and understanding of my needs that made the difference. It was also about making me feel like I belonged out there on the course and that I was not an imposter.

Sometimes, we can't pinpoint where our confidence came from, but we can identify when it is permanently damaged. To illustrate my point, I'll present the other side, one of my confidence vampires.

The Door Holder

In keeping with the theme of grade school sports, I can pinpoint a moment when my confidence was drained, and why today I still have to fight an internal dialogue. It was in sixth grade gym class. Up until that point, my athletic ability wasn't something I thought about. However, once I was in middle school, the expectations concerning athleticism were suddenly a measure of your value. I proudly showed up to gym every day in my cool pink tennis shoes until the day I learned that I didn't belong.

Coach Marco was our Leader, a rather gruff woman who favored the athletically gifted students. The day it happened we were instructed to run lines in the gym; run to the first line, run back, run to the second, run back, etc.

> **WE HAVE HIGH ANXIETY OVER THE OUTCOMES IF WE HAVE A LOW SENSE OF AGENCY. AND WE HAVE LOW ANXIETY IF WE HAVE A HIGH SENSE OF AGENCY.**

Coach Marco commanded all the students to form two lines, the fast students in the front and the slow ones in the back. Unaware of my classification, I got in the front. With an audience of the entire grade, she bellowed,

"Cié, you are the slowest kid in school; get to the back."

This, of course, was followed by laughter and insults from the students. From that day on I was labeled the slowest runner and have carried that with me into adulthood. Hence choosing golf due to lack of running, and still worrying about being last in CrossFit. It was a thought that found a home in my subconscious and would not leave.

Does this mean I never ran again? No. I have completed two half-marathons, but the difference is that the confidence needs to be coaxed out every single time. In anything that requires running, my mind immediately goes to me being the slowest, and I must actively work at telling myself that it's okay, that no one is judging me; *I'm an adult for goodness sake!* It takes an inordinate amount of energy to reframe. This is quite different from my attitude toward golf where my mind is just excited to play, and the outcome doesn't bother me.

We have high anxiety over the outcomes if we have a low sense of Agency. And we have low anxiety if we have a high sense of Agency. I have a high sense of Agency when it comes to golf and a low sense of Agency when it comes to running.

Coach Bradford was a Door Holder.

Coach Marco was not.

Which one do you want to be? A better question is, which one are you right now? As a Door Holder, you can help in vanquishing these confidence vampires, thus helping to increase Agency. Who was a Coach Bradford for you and who was Coach Marco? What Coach Marco from a past work environment is still holding on to you or your team members' confidence?

A way to help move beyond negative past work experiences is by mapping it out. The ability to articulate it clearly allows for understanding and a path toward reframing it. The following process can assist in getting to the source of confidence deficits.

Describe it in detail. Think about a troubling confidence event. Pinpoint the moment you became impacted. Unpack this. Was it the situation or a person(s) that caused the emotion? For example, if Coach Marco had said I was the slowest student in the sixth grade privately, it may not have stuck with me as much as it did because it was said in a public setting.

Who was involved? What were the power dynamics (peers or supervisors)? Sometimes, a toxic environment isn't toxic because the vampire bites are directed at you. It may be directed at others, and you are simply caught in the experience.

How long ago did this take place? My Coach Marco event took place many years ago, and yes, I still get those voices of self-doubt about running. That's why I convinced myself I was going to faint at CrossFit. My self-doubt took control. If you are still impacted by something from years ago, you must commit the time to reframing it.

It is okay to allow for a time to be upset, but you must have an end date. If you do not move on, that confidence vampire is still in control. Stop letting other people (or the past) steal your power.

What were the emotions? What emotions were created from that incident? What aspects of your new employment are similar? Different? What triggers you now in your current role? As an example, I was embarrassed in the sixth grade, that embarrassment resurfaces when I'm in a situation where I'm running with a group of people.

What would you have done differently? If you understand how to handle a situation differently, you will feel more prepared to address it if something similar happens again.

Reframe your reflection. Change "*Why did this happen TO me?*" to "*Why did this happen FOR me?*" Coach Marco taught me a Leadership lesson of how devastating even just a few words can be. I try to be self-aware of my words to others and understand how fragile confidence can be for some. Remember, we are all walking different paths and we are all dealing with different types of hurdles.

> "It's not the event that make us unhappy, it's the way we think about it. The event is not recurring over and over, it's in the past, but we choose to give it life in how we think about it."
>
> –Mo Gawdat

The best way to heal a team from a past toxic environment is to deploy the strategies from Chapters 2 through 5 and build confidence. Let's discuss a few pointers on how you can start building confidence in others.

Start with a conversation. Ask what areas people would like to grow. This will help you understand where your support is needed. You may also discover that people feel deficient in an area they are in fact skilled in, so perhaps more specific praise is needed.

Some phases to boost confidence include:
- I have confidence in you.
- This is what I want us to accomplish (then explain your ideas and be the map for the process).
- I'm interested in utilizing your strengths.
- I'd love to get your opinion on this.
- Debate this with me and help me see what I'm missing.

Be aware of the professional situation. You understand how experiencing something new can shake our confidence. It is also important to understand that everyone approaches something new differently. You may not always know if someone is having anxiety because they may not tell you. Put practices into place to mitigate stressful occurrences before they have a chance to start.

Be aware of employees who are in new situations and construct and/or strengthen channels for engaging in open dialogue. Make sure that you can be a support structure if needed. Instead of merely asking *how's it going*, ask deeper questions, like:

"Have you encountered any roadblocks?"

"I'd love your feedback on what's going well and where we have growth opportunities."

Allow failing forward. Let people fail without making them feel like a failure. Mistakes are going to happen because no one is perfect. Take a mistake and make it a learning moment, not a shameful one. We will delve more into failing forward in Chapter 7.

Set the expectations. Everyone has different time management skills. When giving something new that is in addition to their normal load, take the time to have a conversation with them about how they will fit it into their schedule. This lets the team member know that you understand their workload and want to work with them to help them be successful.

Train. It's hard to feel confident in something you haven't been trained in. When you place unexpressed expectations on someone, you are the one setting yourself up to feel let down.

This has happened to me. I was brand new in a role when this texting interaction unfolded.

Cié, I'm out till next week… I forgot to send the prospect email, can you do it?

I don't know how to use the database yet to pull the targeted addresses.

You can figure it out it's not hard.

I'm concerned about sending 50,000 emails incorrectly since I haven't been trained on the system, is there anyone available to show me?

Part of training and coaching means understanding the skill or exposure level of the other person. It may not be hard if you understand the system. Set people up for success. In the texting exchange described, I never received a reply and I did the email merge wrong!

Trust. Display trust in others. Instead of canceling a meeting because you have a conflict, try saying to your talented employee, "I cannot make the meeting, but I have full confidence in your ability to lead it. Let me know if you have any questions before the meeting. Thank you so much."

Trust deserves more than a couple of sentences, so let's dive deeper and talk about the confidence to trust.

CONFIDENCE TO TRUST

If you have created an environment where your team cannot function without immediate supervision, there will eventually be a problem. If you hold information so your team is required to check in with you to make decisions or get work done, there will be issues. Teams need confidence, autonomy, and a chance to use their skills to be able to adapt to unexpected situations and make decisions. You aren't going to hold the Door and they aren't going to walk through it if there is not trust.

> **IF YOU HAVE CREATED AN ENVIRONMENT WHERE YOUR TEAM CANNOT FUNCTION WITHOUT IMMEDIATE SUPERVISION, THERE WILL EVENTUALLY BE A PROBLEM.**

A POMPOUS CIRCUMSTANCE

Early in my career, I organized university graduation ceremonies for about 3,000 students a semester. I did this position for many years and was so effective I could predict when something might go wrong and head it off at the pass. Eventually, I grew from an entry-level position to leading the office, which mandated a need to cross-train others in this role. But my attachment to control was very strong.

At each ceremony I would begrudgingly give away small duties to my staff of two young professionals. However, I stubbornly held the ownership of the important tasks. Finally, I decided to turn over the coveted role of on-stage activities to my team. I was nervous. This was a live event with 10,000 people in the audience and thousands of students. If it went poorly, our office would be seen in a bad light. *I would be* seen in a bad light. But I trained them, they shadowed the ceremonies, and they were ready.

The ceremony began. I stood off to the side, peeking through the curtain while the two staff got into position. The university band began *Pomp and Circumstance*, and the graduates started moving. I looked at one of the staff and noticed a slight hint of confusion about what to do. I panicked, ripped back the curtain, and pushed her to the side so I could take over. Yes, I physically pushed her out of the way. I still remember the utter confusion, embarrassment, and disappointment on her face.

What did that do to her confidence? What did that do to the trust in our professional relationship? Why did I have such a hard time letting go and trusting someone else?

If we have a problem letting go or delegating, we might be holding on to one of the myths about delegation.[46] These can almost be unconscious beliefs that we are unaware of until we pause and reflect. Which of these are you guilty of?

The myth of diminished authority. We believe we will not be seen as the authority figure if other people are doing tasks that we used to do. There are some tasks that define our roles, for example, the graduation ceremony was (at least in my mind) a pivotal role that defined my authority in the organi-

> **YOU ARE NOT MORE OF A LEADER IF YOU HOARD ALL THE WORK, YOUR AUTHORITY ACTUALLY DIMINISHES.**

---

46. Bhasin, Hitesh. "8 Myths About Delegation Managers Should Be Aware Of." *Marketing91*, June 9, 2023. Accessed June 9, 2023. https://www.marketing91.com/8-myths-delegation-managers-aware/.

The Door Holder

zation. If someone else does our 'pivotal task' we may feel our authority is diminished.

FALSE.

As a Leader, your authority comes from your ability to coach others, remove obstacles, and support their growth. Your authority becomes diminished if you hoard all the work. Your authority comes from your ability to open Doors. I could have been a Door Holder in this graduation example. Instead, I just slammed and locked it.

The myth of incompetence. We believe if someone else does OUR job, it looks like we were replaced and thus are incapable. Instead of seeing the positive view of cross training and allowing others to experience new tasks, we can sometimes see it as a threat to our competence. We are concerned about appearances of how it will look if we are no longer doing it.

FALSE.

You are assigned as the Leader of the team, rather than the person doing all the duties of the team. The struggle with feelings of incompetence goes back to self-doubt and those negative internal messages. Taking time to explore that can help you move forward.

The myth that my way is best. We believe that no one can do it better than we can. Whether we choose to admit it or not, we have all held this notion that our way is the only way that works.

FALSE.

This is especially true with something you have worked on for a long time or created yourself from scratch. Like my graduation example, I owned it, everyone knew I owned it, and it was very difficult letting others own some of that process. But in retrospect, new people had great new ideas. I'm not in that area any longer, and if I hadn't delegated and cross-trained, it would have suffered when I left. Why would I hurt the team doing all the work just so I could say *Ta-da, I did it*!

The myth of mistrust. The belief that your team cannot fully be trusted to deliver quality outcomes. We can't trust that anyway is better than ours, or that our team members will succeed.

FALSE.

We often are apprehensive about trust. WHY? Exploring the different reasons you may have an issue with trust will help you make a plan to improve it.

- ▸ If you don't trust because you feel there is a lack of knowledge, train.
- ▸ If you don't trust because you feel they won't be able to do a task or because it has been done poorly in the past, go back to Chapter 3 on growth and have a conversation about performance expectations and growth

opportunities. Analyze how you are explaining the deliverables, perhaps your instructions are not clear.
- If you don't feel you can trust because they do not have the confidence to perform, re-read this chapter.
- If you don't feel you can trust, but you don't have any specific reasons, ask yourself why? If there is no real evidence that they can't or won't do a task, reframe your internal conversation. Make a plan to ease yourself and the team member into owning something. Be careful not to drag past experiences into a current role and project a lack of trust. Make sure you aren't affected by an old vampire.

The myth of time. We believe it will take too much time to train someone. The workload is too intense therefore taking precious time to coach and develop someone else is simply not possible. We also believe that people don't want to learn something new, everyone is just too busy. It's working the way it is now, why change anything?

FALSE.

A Leader who hoards all the work will eventually crumble. Either from a lack of time to listen to new ideas or a need for more attention to the changing landscape of their field. This results in stagnant practices, no innovation, and a staff that operates like drones. As for everyone being too busy, there is value in doing a task inventory to see what people are spending their time on that really doesn't matter. Some things are just historical tasks that everyone thinks they must do.

The myth that we will delegate ourselves out of a job. We believe we will pass all our work off to others and have nothing to do. Therefore, we will become obsolete and be fired.

FALSE.

If done correctly, you will create a cohesive, high-performing team. By delegating you will have time to work more on cultivation and holding the Door rather than trying to do all your team members' jobs for them.

Trust is like making caramel sauce. I like to spend my holiday break experimenting with baking. I fail a lot in my culinary endeavors, but I also learn a lot. One holiday season I was making a Japanese pudding that required a caramel sauce. I had never made a caramel sauce before. It's sugar and water. How hard can that be?

The instructions clearly said, "Bring to a boil, but do not stir."

I stirred.

The urge to stir was too great. I literally could not stop myself from stirring the pot. What resulted was a hard sugar mess.

So, I tried again, this time not stirring. The desire to intervene was great and I had to make myself just step back and watch until the mixture turned the correct deep golden color.

It worked. I put the right ingredients together, set the right temperature, and watched it, but left it alone, and it worked all on its own without my help. If we put the right people together with the right resources, support, and guidance, set the right temperature (climate), and trust them to do the work, it will happen. But if we can't resist jumping in to stir the pot, success will be slow going.

Before we end our chapter on confidence, I wanted to finish the story about the Leadership development program that I began this chapter with. The one in which I was sure I'd be kicked out because I didn't belong and was conflicted about what fork to use.

At the end of that year-long program, I was voted in by my peers as a lead for the next year's programming – *The peers with higher titles and more advanced degrees.* The first year I led was the year the speaker canceled, and I had to fill in for the entire day (the day I had to use my Agency that was revealed to you in the preface of this book).

The next year, I was promoted to lead facilitator of the program and I held that role for ten years.

But there's a twist.

About five years into the program, I found out that I was not the first choice for nomination. Someone else was nominated but they had to back out, so I was a last-minute substitution. Originally, I wasn't even supposed to be there. By the time I found this out I had already done so much internal work to muzzle and reframe my self-doubt that this new knowledge didn't affect me. If I had not put a conscious effort in to reframing negative distortions, I may have crumbled at this realization that I was in fact never supposed to be in that program.

THOUGHTS TO CONSIDER

- No one sees the version of you that you see yourself.
- You are never the only one dealing with lack of confidence.
- When you start talking negatively about yourself, imagine saying those things about the person closest to you (your child, parent, partner, or best friend).
- A lot of our cognitive distress is over things that don't even exist.
- Having a growth mindset can help identify negative internal dialogue and reframe it.
- Don't be a confidence vampire sucking the life out of your team.
- You are already enough.

"Always remember you are braver than you believe, stronger than you seem, and smarter than you think."

—CHRISTOPHER ROBIN

Chapter 7

Y IS FOR YOU

> "If you want to improve the organization you have to improve yourself and the organization gets pulled up with you."
>
> — Indra Nooyi, former CEO PepsiCo

Referring back to the CrossFit story, when I thought I was going to faint and it was just a piece of floor on my sweaty face, I want to ask you a question: **What is the piece of floor on your face?** What is keeping you from growing, evolving, and moving to be the Leader that inspires, motivates, and holds the Door? What do you need to do to build your own Agency?

This chapter is about why YOU are reading this book. You want to be a better Leader. But the word **better** is in the eye of the beholder. You are the one that must determine **how** you need or want to improve.

I've mentioned our old friend **time** throughout this book. Many of the activities such as relationship building, growth cultivation, and listening require time. We all love instant gratification. The check box is often seen as the quick fix. Please don't get to the end of this book and neglect to implement any of the ideas suggested. Anything worth doing is worth putting in the time to do it right. So, let's talk about YOU.

You can't help others until you help yourself.

You can't open the Door for others if you are afraid to fail.

You can't develop Agency if you don't have emotional intelligence.

This last chapter will navigate us through these three main ideas to leave you with a complete playbook on how to navigate the art of Leadership and become the Door Holder.

OXYGEN MASK

What is part of the flight attendant's safety instructions on the airplane? Put your own mask on first before helping those around you. How often do we practice this in our work contexts? Do you have your own Leadership oxygen mask?

Taking time to make sure your needs are met and that you are in a good Leadership headspace sometimes takes a backseat as we try to accomplish all we are required and/or accountable to do. Our lack of attention to our own basic needs often sneaks up on us. It's like toast in the toaster. We feel the need to do more, so we set the temperature high,

> **YOU CAN'T HOLD THE DOOR IF YOU ARE A BURNT PIECE OF TOAST.**

only to end up just getting burned. You can't hold the Door if you are a burnt piece of toast.

Let's review some well-known, but frequently ignored actionable steps you can take today to start meeting your needs, or at least start assessing what your needs are.

Get up. Sitting for long periods of time increases our chances for seriously harmful conditions, including anxiety, blood clots, and weight gain, to name just a few. I'm not a medical doctor, so I won't go deep into this, but please remember to move about and stay active.

Eat healthy. I'll be honest. I used to get mad when I'd look for ways to improve, and the answer was to eat better. But after I started getting acid reflux and wanting to take a nap every day at 3:00 p.m. after my candy bar snack, I changed my habits. The food we choose affects our mood, productivity, energy levels, and mental clarity.

Get enough sleep. Lack of sleep affects brain function, weakens immunity, increases the likelihood of depression, and makes you moody. Some reading this may think you cannot get ahead without working into the wee hours of the morning. I can honestly say I get a solid seven to eight hours of sleep every night.

Learn to let stuff go. I'm not talking about delegation of tasks (although that's important). I'm talking about the mental thoughts we choose to cling to; the ones that come in the middle of the night, causing us to not get enough sleep. Take the lessons learned but let the rest go.

Take time off. I promise the office will be there when you get back. The most startling and humbling experience I ever had was when I had a conference one week, and then I got sick and had to miss another week, so I was gone for two weeks. Everything was fine; nothing fell apart.

Taking time off and still checking emails doesn't count because your mind isn't on vacation with you. Remember to pack your mind in your suitcase too.

Set boundaries. As the Leader, we are often called upon to solve issues or get drawn into personal issues or task completion micromanaging. Set boundaries with staff so they respect your time as much as you respect theirs.

Value your mental health. Meditate, talk with a counselor, keep a journal, take walks, whatever you need to do, do it. There is no shame in admitting that you are struggling in an area. We all struggle.

Speak up. Whatever it is, if you feel your voice needs to be heard, make it heard. Arrange a meeting with the appropriate person and let them know you need to have a serious conversation. Set the expectations that you need their attention, guidance, advice, whatever is appropriate for the situation. People aren't mind readers; sometimes we have to be inescapably clear.

Now that we have those basic needs covered, let's get into the heart of YOU. How's that relationship with failure going?

FUN WITH FAILURE

It's not encouraging to start a chapter about YOU with failure. This is a scary word that needs some serious reframing. When I've given workshops on Leadership, the most common negative phrase uttered, especially from new Leaders, is *what if I fail?*

What's your definition of failure? You, as a Leader of a team, organization, group, project, or whatever, are responsible for success. But what does success look like?

We can get so wrapped up in our possible failures that our view of reality becomes clouded. If we sit down and draw out what failure really looks like, taking it from the generic absolute to a tangible definition, we would be surprised.

We also carry failures from the past with us. If I carried all the times I earned a bad grade on a written piece, was rejected from a publication, or received the *no thanks* letter for a Leadership proposal I submitted, I would have never written this book.

> **IT'S HARD TO HOLD THE DOOR FOR OTHERS TO GROW FROM FAILURE UNTIL YOU FIRST KNOW HOW TO GROW FROM FAILURE YOURSELF.**

It's hard to hold the Door for others to grow from failure until you first know how to grow from failure yourself.

MEMORY LANE

In 2019, I had the pleasure of taking my former public speaking professor out to lunch to celebrate his retirement. When I arrived at the Communication Department to meet him, he handed me a packet. While cleaning out his desk, and thirty years of accumulated student artifacts, he found photos of me from 1999 and 2000 when I represented the university as an undergraduate in speech competitions. If that wasn't enough of a throwback, he also had the transcripts of my speeches. You may assume I was entertained by a walk down memory lane. You are incorrect. Although it had been twenty years, I immediately felt the cold slap of failure and rejection. It was visceral to the point of giving me a stomachache.

In 1999, I was an undergraduate Communication major. The city held an annual speech competition that invited local college students to compete by presenting a ten-minute memorized discourse on Texas history. While some might consider this event their worst nightmare, I was ecstatic. I entered for the first time in 1999 and was awarded fourth place and $400.

Moderately pleased, I was eager to try again the next year as I now had experience and knew what to expect. As soon as the new topic was announced for the 2000 competition, I hit the ground running. My research was more intense, and I rehearsed for hours in front of a home video camera acting as my own coach and critic. On the day of the competition, full of confidence and a bit of arrogance, I performed my speech.

Feeling narcissistic with satisfaction, I sat impatiently for the rest of the speakers to finish so I could receive my award and allow the celebration to commence. But the celebration never came. My name was never called. I did not even place in the top five. Disappointment overwhelmed me as I accepted condolences from my professor and provided forced congratulatory remarks to my superior competitors. Awkwardly fleeing the scene, I managed to make it to my car before bursting into tears.

First, as a self-coping mechanism, I rationalized how it wasn't my fault through conspiracy theory and projected blame.

It was rigged!

They were passing the award around for political reasons.

The other competitors had connections that I didn't have.

Then came the feelings of inadequacy and self-loathing.

I'm a failure at public speaking.

I failed my institution.

I failed my professor.

I graduated college that spring and thus, my dream of becoming a Speech Champion was never realized. Obviously, this event didn't squash my public speaking career, but I have always carried with me the sentiment that I failed.

After lunch with my professor, I hurried back to my office to begin reading the old transcripts of the speeches. I began with the fourth place speech. I found it a bit simplistic, but it was factual and told an entertaining story. I decided it was fourth place material and the judges were correct in their evaluation. Then, I began to read the dreaded failed speech. As I finally reached the very last line, I sat back in my chair and laughed out loud.

The speech…was…terrible!

There was no consistency, no flow, and basically just a regurgitation of facts. I had not synthesized the information nor made it enjoyable to listen to, and there was no identifiable conclusion! I finally understood why I didn't place. I was surprised at my feeling of intense relief. There was no self-loathing or regret, only the blissful understanding that it wasn't my best work. I didn't deserve to win and that was okay. However, the true source of my relief (twenty years later) was knowing that this little failed speech was only a tiny bump in the road, and it didn't stop me from pushing myself forward. It was also proof that somewhere along my journey I had developed a growth mindset. *Thank goodness.*

The ability to analyze one's professional performance with high emotional intelligence and an objective eye is sometimes difficult. I cannot say that even now, I never have moments of self-doubt or inflated confidence. However, I am much more cognizant and can manage high emotions to find meaning and growth opportunities. Therefore, no matter how many times I fail, I will always win. Reflecting on this experience made me realize several lessons about failure.

Confidence is important, but overconfidence can be a hindrance. We spent a whole section of this book talking about building confidence. But if we are too confident, or arrogant, or refuse to acknowledge growth opportunities, we can falter. It comes down to understanding who you are and how you operate. We must be cautious not to be blind to our growth opportunities. I chose to ignore any growth opportunities from the 1999 speech.

Let failure fuel your Agency to better destinations. If we operate from a fixed mindset, we will sit with our failure and let it trick us into thinking, *this is it; this is as far as you can go*. Through a growth mindset perspective, you can move ahead. If you are a check box person, check off that you just found another way how NOT to do something.

Learn from others. If the only feedback you are getting is from yourself, it's a problem. This has always been a tough one for me. Early on, I viewed any negative feedback as a dig at me as a human being. It takes emotional intelligence (which we will discuss in a bit) and an openness to improve in order to handle or process feedback correctly and beneficially. It also takes critical analysis. Not all feedback may seem beneficial or even relevant at the time. Taking time to review, listen, and reflect can help categorize the areas that the feedback pertains to.

An example of this is when I presented my dissertation results at a conference. I expected to learn from the evaluations what the audience thought about my research or presentation skills. One comment completely took me off guard.

My dissertation was on the advancement of senior-level women in higher education and the microaggressions/stereotypes they had to navigate. In my presentation, I made a snide remark about a female reality show celebrity. I do not remember why that comment even made it

> **THE OUTCOME ISN'T ALWAYS THE MEASUREMENT OF SUCCESS. SOMETIMES SUCCESS LIES IN THE GROWTH AND LEARNING.**

from my brain to my mouth as it had nothing to do with my presentation. In the evaluation, the audience member called out that I was being a hypocrite. How can I promote the empowerment of women and in the same breath, tear a woman down? They were absolutely correct.

My first instinct was to reject that comment, but after reflection, I understood what it meant in the bigger picture of how I presented myself and my message.

Sometimes, hard work doesn't render the intended results. We will all put a thousand hours into something that fails. It is only sometimes the outcome that is the measure of growth and learning. Agency means being able to manage whatever outcome may result.

Don't dwell in the gray wasteland of ambiguity for too long. We will *fail*, and we may never know the real reason why. For example, in my experience about not even placing in the speech competition, I only have my interpretation of the value of my speech, I will never really know why I didn't win. When we don't get the job or get passed for the promotion or our presentation falls flat, uncertainty reduction is what we want. We either blame ourselves or others to find some kind of answer when there could be an infinite number of reasons. Find the golden nuggets of wisdom and move on.

Constant self-reflection on your progress as a Leader is critical. In cleaning out my own file cabinet, I came across a list of previous failures I was asked to jot down for a workshop. I do not remember this workshop, but the failures are crystal clear.

Looking at the noted FAILURES, I remember #1, "Didn't get that job." I was gutted when I didn't get that *dream job*. I interviewed for two months and made a site visit. The only thing I got was the 'thanks but we are going with another candidate' email. #2 has already been discussed in how I let my health deteriorate. I deemed that a major failure. And #3 is more personal, "Living someone else's life." I grew up in an

FAILURE
Write down three times you have failed.

1. Didn't get 'THAT' job

2. Health

3. Living someone else's life

WHAT YOU LEARNED FROM YOUR FAILURES

WISDOM

1. Grass is not greener. My skills are good, but I don't fit everywhere

2. get out what you put in

3. Define my identity + own it

adverse environment and had numerous restrictions placed on me because of this association. My mother was mentally ill, and for many years, I felt a sense of shame and blame for her actions and behaviors. Looking at the WISDOM side, #1, I realized that dream job wasn't perfect, and better opportunities came along. It wasn't failure, it was redirection. For #2, I can't expect to just be healthy by proclamation, I now know the work that has to be put forth. Sometimes we need failure to wake us up (my story about blacking out in the classroom). #3 is honestly sometimes still a struggle, trying to define my identity and not living someone else's. But I know how far I've come at gaining closure on several of those past experiences. In this example, I'm not a failure because of someone else's issue, I had to reframe my thinking. There is Agency in owning your own identity and making changes in your environment. There is Agency in reflecting on your perceived failures and finding the positive outcomes.

This worksheet was a glimpse into what having Agency can do. It shows how it can change your perception of yourself, your views on perceived failure, and how you have the ability to grow.

I've stated over and over that Leadership is a journey. Everything we have discussed so far in this book, whether you are improving yourself or holding the Door for others, takes time and reflection. Wisdom and clarity take time. Be patient with yourself, it will come.

> "The greatest teacher failure is."
>
> YODA

Who is Looking Back in your Mirror? Agency is cultivated through our experiences and involves intrapersonal communication, such as intentionality in planning, forethought, self-reactiveness, and self-reflectiveness.[47]

The aspect of becoming the Door Holder that is most easily pushed to the end of the priority list is self-reflection. The day is simply filled with too much noise and there isn't enough precious time to waste on thinking. We are all living at a critical time where Leaders must provoke a certain degree of reflection, which includes understanding their purpose and core values and taking the time to emotionally evaluate.[48]

Self-reflection is taking time to observe yourself and your thoughts without judgment. It's not a time to pick yourself apart or find fault. It's about understanding your thought processes, taking the time to assess your feelings about various situations and experiences, and processing your environment.

Self-reflection can help us identify our default emotions. Default emotions are those emotions that we fall into automatically during difficult situations. Maybe it's anxiety or fear. But that may be an emotion that is hiding a different emotion. Susan David describes emotional umbrellas as emotions that can be masking other emotions.[49]

Here is an example of an umbrella emotion. In the past, when faced with a situation where I didn't know the answer,

---

47. Bandura, "Exercise of Human Agency"
48. Edmondson, Amy C., Richard E. Boyatzis, Aaron De Smet, and Bill Schaninger. "Psychological Safety, Emotional Intelligence, and Leadership in a Time of Flux." *McKinsey Quarterly* 3 (2020): 1–6.
49. David, "Emotional Granularity Umbrellas"

I would default to the emotion of anger. It was physiological. I would get hot; my heart would race. But what was really going on was defensiveness. I was defensive that someone would perceive me as incompetent. I have done a lot of self-reflection to explore this fear. Now, I approach those ambiguous situations calmly because I know it's okay not to know everything.

The conversations we have with ourselves are very critical in becoming a better Leader. We have more power to shape outcomes than we believe, and with this power we can shape them positively instead of negatively. We have much more control over our situations than we realize. For example, a self-fulfilling prophecy is when an individual's expectation of an event helps create the very condition that permits that event to happen.[50] The scenario below will explain this phenomenon.

Pretend you were invited to a party. You formed an internal expectation that the party would be boring, and no one would talk to you. Perhaps these beliefs grew out of an emotion of anxiety because you didn't know anyone, or felt awkward at large gatherings. You arrive at the party and your non-verbal language emulates your thoughts. Your arms are crossed, and you look bored and unapproachable. People at the party respond to these cues, adjusting their behavior to match. The result is you end up being bored and no one talks to you. Thus, you have fulfilled your prophecy.

---

50 Biggs, Michael A. "Prophecy, Self-Fulfilling/Self-Defeating." In *Encyclopedia of Philosophy and the Social Sciences*, edited by Byron Kaldis. Thousand Oaks, CA: SAGE Publications, 2013.

In Leadership, it is also very easy to create expectations of events in our heads that can go toward the negative. Unconsciously, we are sometimes steering the outcome to match these expectations. Perhaps you believe the constructive feedback conversation will go poorly, so your body language and how you respond with tone reinforces your pessimism to a negative outcome.

Set your expectations to the positive. In our party example, form an expectation that you will meet interesting people and have a good time. When you arrive at the party, your body language will match this optimism with a smile and approachable demeanor. People will respond to these cues, adjusting their behavior to match. The result is that you will, most likely, talk to people and fulfill a much different prophecy. Understanding what drives our thoughts, actions, and reactions involves a skill we have all heard of but may struggle with to apply consistently – emotional intelligence.

EMOTIONAL INTELLIGENCE

Emotional intelligence is our ability to manage, understand, and handle our emotions.[51] This can mean emotions from failure or the threat of failure. The ability to manage our emotions opens the Door for us to be self-reflective and honest with ourselves. People with high emotional intelligence can recognize not only their

> **SOME LEADERS OPERATE IN A SURVIVALIST DYSTOPIAN SCENARIO WHERE TRUST ISN'T AN OPTION AND EVERYONE IS OUT FOR THEMSELVES.**

---

51. Goleman, Daniel. "What Makes a Leader?" *Harvard Business Review* 76, no. 6 (1998): 92–105.

own emotions, but also those of others. To be a Door Holder, one must possess high emotional intelligence. But what does that mean? This is not a new term and one I'm sure you have heard of or even had training on. However, emotional intelligence has several components that Door Holders must be aware of and thus warrants a revisit. Self-awareness, self-regulation, motivation, and our old friend empathy are critical skills to building Agency and holding the Door.

Self-Awareness is having a deep understanding of one's emotions, strengths, weaknesses, needs, and drives. Of the many Door slammers that I have encountered in my life, it is my perception that the most significant reason for their inability to lift others up is their own lack of self-awareness of emotions and drives. When I shoved my team member out of the way so I could take over the university graduation, I was grossly un self-aware. I was so unaware that it didn't even register to me that I did anything wrong until after the ceremony when she approached me with tears in her eyes and asked for a conversation.

Some Leaders are too fixated on selfish promotion or one-upping someone else. Others are driven by fear or the drive to prove someone wrong. Some operate in a survivalist dystopian scenario where trust isn't an option and everyone is out for themselves. The ability to take a hard look at yourself and see how your actions are helping or hurting those in your charge is paramount to every Leader's success.

Self-Regulation is the ability to control or re-direct disruptive impulses. As I've stated before, being the Door Holder comes with responsibility and a good amount of work. I also stated we are not robots, and that our emotions and impulses play a large part in our workplace interactions. Being able to regulate or re-direct our impulses will help achieve patience and make better decisions that will support the Door Holder philosophy.

Motivation is the passion to work for reasons that go beyond money or status. If we are only concerned with the prestige of our title or the amount of money we earn, we will miss the mark when it comes to Leading. When we are only motivated by selfish reasons, how does that translate into holding the Door for others? Motivation lives in a growth mindset where we are optimistic about reaching our goals, take opportunities when they come, and enjoy our work.

Empathy, as discussed in Chapter 4, is understanding the emotional makeup of others. Sometimes, we need to have empathy with ourselves. Empathy is a way to change the perception or recategorize past events.

Yes, it is hard to empathize with a nasty personality, but you never know the personal monsters people are battling. The important thing to consider is that negativity comes from inside the person. It's created inside them and then pushed out at you. You didn't create it; you were just the unfortunate recipient. Emotional intelligence allows us to see this and thoughtfully manage it.

If you are reading this wondering if you are emotionally intelligent or not, here are a few signs of emotional intelligence (adapted from Bradberry).[52]

---

52. Bradberry, Travis. "18 Signs You Have High Emotional Intelligence." *Success*, January 5, 2024. Accessed January 5, 2024. https://www.success.com/18-signs-you-have-high-emotional-intelligence/.

You have an emotional vocabulary. The greater the range of terms and meanings that we use to describe internal states, the easier it is to identify how we feel and trace this feeling to its emotional source. This is also important when communicating with your team.

For example, I told you I would get mad when I felt my competence was being questioned. Now that I have a broader emotional vocabulary, I know that I'm not mad, but rather, depending on the situation, I am really feeling:

Scared because I may not have prepared as much as I should.

Defensive because this person always seems to question me.

Embarrassed because I really don't have the answer.

A stronger emotional vocabulary gives you a broader canvas to paint on and thus more scenery to understand the real picture.

You are empathetically curious about other people. It's not about passing judgment on others but rather approaching situations with curiosity and a desire to understand. When we understand the reasons behind another's actions, we can approach situations with more clarity. Don't fill the void with your own meaning.

You can adapt. We know that Agency is the belief that you have the capacity to make a change. Emotional intelligence allows us to manage any perceived threats of an outcome. We can adapt, rather we KNOW we can adapt to whatever may come.

You understand your strengths and weaknesses, and you don't get all bent out of shape about them. By understanding where we are strong and admitting where we are weak, we will do those strengths with confidence and not try to fake our way through our weaknesses.

You are socially aware. You have the ability to understand where people are coming from and what may be driving their actions/reactions.

You understand that "No" is a complete sentence. You have the boundary-setting capabilities to communicate 'no' with empathy and not be bullied into saying 'yes.'

You approach situations with positive intent. Give others the benefit of the doubt. Assume that they have good intentions and approach situations with this mindset. Choose your words carefully and use positive language when communicating. Avoid accusatory or judgmental language.

You take care of yourself. You monitor your needs by disconnecting, eating healthy, getting enough sleep, and avoiding burnout.

In a final thought on YOU: Why did you read this book? *(You are almost finished, by the way. Exceptional job in sticking with it!)*

Do you want to be a Door Holder, or are you drawn more to the Line Leader? You have probably figured out by now (because you are awesome and smart) the reality is that we need both in a balance. Leadership is a dance, and we change positions as we go, sometimes leading, sometimes following. It only becomes a problem when we stop moving, ignore our partner, or prefer to dance alone in the spotlight. The Door Holder philosophy is a mindset and a form of wisdom to understand when to hold the Door for others and when to walk through and Lead so others can follow.

K2

To inject greater impact on the messages in this book and tie them up in one nice ending story, I'd like to take you far away from conference rooms and Zoom calls.

Nirmal (Nims) Purja is a mountaineer from Nepal who gained notoriety for climbing the fourteen tallest mountains in the world in six months and six days. He was not attempting this herculean feat for his own notoriety; rather, it was for recognition of the Nepalese sherpas. We know the names of many Western mountaineers who have scaled some of the world's tallest peaks, but we rarely, if ever, hear recognition for the guides – the sherpas that lead the way. Nims named this effort Project **Possible** because everyone told him it was **im**possible. This story focuses on his tenth mountain, K2, the second-highest mountain on Earth located on the China-Pakistan border in the Karakoram Range of the Himalayas.

Nims and his team of Nepalese climbers arrived at K2 base camp.[53] The valley was dotted with yellow and orange tents that strikingly stood out against the gray stone and patches of snow. The climate was somber with the absence of talking or gear prepping, only the howl of the wind and whipping of tents could be heard. Every climb that had been

---

53. *14 Peaks: Nothing Is Impossible.* Directed by Torquil Jones. London: Noah Media Group, Little Monster Films, Presence, 2021. Netflix.

attempted in the last several days was met with failure in the form of avalanches. Nims arrived as the climbers were trying to make a decision to give it one more attempt or scrap this season entirely. The mountain was simply not cooperating.

Rather than lamenting and fixating on the go versus no-go debate, Nims decided to throw a party.

There was a serious decision to be made, a life-or-death decision, but first, Nims wanted to meet everyone and relieve some of the stress. Suddenly, the tents were lit from the glow of campfires with laughter, song, and drink. Nims knew he couldn't burst on the scene and start talking logistics until he understood where these people came from and what they had been through.

The next morning, Nims visited with all the climbers about their concerns over the safety of the mountain. Eyes were filled with fear and an acceptance of defeat that this season's climb would not work. He listened to everyone, even the skeptics and nah-sayers.

Then he got down to the specifics of the problem.

The main hazard was a bottleneck section, which is the crux of the route to the top. There was a giant ice cliff that hung over. Sometimes, it released, resulting in an avalanche that could sweep a whole team down the mountain. It was risky to set the climbing lines (a fixed rope bolted into place to assist climbers). The problem was that setting the lines in daylight was risky since the sun had warmed the ice shelf. The temperatures were the lowest in the middle of the night at 1:00 a.m., which made the snow like concrete. Nims knew what he had to do.

He commented that, as a Leader, you must present yourself with as much confidence as possible. He knew the risks, threats, and challenges. He was even dealing with his own self-doubt. As he spoke to them, he said, "A lot of people have turned around, and a lot of people have failed; we have to unite, and we have to go together."

Starting in the late evening, he and his Nepalese team climbed K2 and reached the ice shelf at its coldest point. They set the lines, then climbed back down to get the team of climbers.

That morning, twenty-four climbers reached the top of K2.

Nims held the Door by creating an environment in which others saw what was possible in themselves. He took time to know them, listen to them, and inspire them. He gave hope, he gave praise, he gave empathy. He Lead the way, then held the Door.

Your mountain is waiting. Who are you bringing with you?

It's your turn; the Door is open.

BIBLIOGRAPHY

14 Peaks: Nothing Is Impossible. Directed by Torquil Jones. London: Noah Media Group, Little Monster Films, Presence, 2021. Netflix.

Adams, Richard. *Watership Down*. New York: Scribner, 1972.

American Psychological Association. "More than a Quarter of U.S. Adults Say They're So Stressed They Can't Function." October 2022. Accessed October 2022. https://www.apa.org/news/press/releases/2022/10/multiple-stressors-no-function.

American Psychological Association. "Stress in America 2020: A National Mental Health Crisis." October 2020. Accessed October 2022. https://www.apa.org/news/press/releases/stress/2020/report-october.

Bandura, Albert. "Exercise of Human Agency through Collective Efficacy." *Psychological Science* 9, no. 3 (2000): 75-78.

Bandura, Albert, and Edwin A. Locke. "Negative Self-Efficacy and Goal Effects Revisited." *Journal of Applied Psychology* 88, no. 1 (2003): 87-99.

Bhasin, Hitesh. "8 Myths About Delegation Managers Should Be Aware Of." *Marketing91*, June 9, 2023. Accessed June 9, 2023. https://www.marketing91.com/8-myths-delegation-managers-aware/.

Biggs, Michael A. "Prophecy, Self-Fulfilling/Self-Defeating." In *Encyclopedia of Philosophy and the Social Sciences*, edited by Byron Kaldis. Thousand Oaks, CA: SAGE Publications, 2013.

Bolden, Richard, Aman Gulati, and Gareth Edwards. "Mobilizing Change in Public Services: Insights from a Systems Leadership Development Intervention." *International Journal of Public Administration* 43, no. 1 (2020): 26-36.

Bradberry, Travis. "18 Signs You Have High Emotional Intelligence." *Success*, January 5, 2024. Accessed January 5, 2024. https://www.success.com/18-signs-you-have-high-emotional-intelligence/.

Brower, Tracy. "Empathy Is the Most Important Leadership Skill." *Forbes*, October 19, 2021. Accessed October 19, 2021. https://www.forbes.com/sites/tracybrower/2021/09/19/empathy-is-the-most-important-leadership-skill-according-to-research/?sh=51c40be33dc5.

Bundy, Jonathan, and Michael D. Pfarrer. "A Burden of Responsibility: The Role of Social Approval at the Onset of a Crisis." *Academy of Management Review* 40, no. 3 (2015): 345-369.

Burns, David D., and Melvin D. Burns. *Feeling Good: The New Mood Therapy*. New York: Signet Books, 1980.

Ciannilli, Michael. "Communication Lessons from the Columbia Tragedy." Presentation at the National Speakers Association Conference, Nashville, TN, 2022.

Clance, Pauline R., and Suzanne A. Imes. "The Impostor Phenomenon in High Achieving Women: Dynamics and Therapeutic Intervention." *Psychotherapy: Theory, Research & Practice* 15, no. 3 (1978): 241–247.

D'Auria, Gianpiero, and Aaron De Smet. "Leadership in a Crisis: Responding to the Coronavirus Outbreak and Future Challenges." March 16, 2020. Accessed March 16, 2020. https://www.mckinsey.com/capabilities/people-and-organizational-performance/our-insights/leadership-in-a-crisis-responding-to-the-coronavirus-outbreak-and-future-challenges#/.

David, Susan. "Emotional Granularity Umbrellas." October 12, 2022. Accessed October 12, 2022. https://www.susandavid.com/resource/emotional-granularity-umbrellas/.

Dill, Bonnie Thornton, Angela E. McLaughlin, and Angela D. Nieves. "Future Directions of Feminist Research: Intersectionality." In *Handbook of Feminist Research*, edited by Sharlene Nagy Hesse-Biber, 629–637. Thousand Oaks, CA: SAGE Publications, 2007.

Dweck, Carol S. Mindset: *The New Psychology of Success.* New York: Ballantine Books, 2007.

Edmondson, Amy C. *The Fearless Organization: Creating Psychological Safety in the Workplace for Learning, Innovation, and Growth.* Hoboken, NJ: John Wiley & Sons, 2019.

Edmondson, Amy C., Richard E. Boyatzis, Aaron De Smet, and Bill Schaninger. "Psychological Safety, Emotional Intelligence, and Leadership in a Time of Flux." *McKinsey Quarterly* 3 (2020): 1–6.

Gee, Cié. "Getting Real 20 Years Later: A Lesson in Failure." AACRAO Connect: Field Notes, 2019.

Gee, Cié. "The Empathetic Leader." AACRAO Connect: Field Notes, January 2022.

Gee, Cié. " Self-Doubt, Lack of Confidence, and Imposter Syndrome in Higher Education Leaders.' AACRAO Connect: Field Notes, July 2022.

Goleman, Daniel. "What Makes a Leader?" *Harvard Business Review* 76, no. 6 (1998): 92–105.

Graham, Jill W. "Servant-Leadership in Organizations: Inspirational and Moral." *The Leadership Quarterly* 2, no. 2 (1991): 105-119.

Greenleaf, Robert K. *Servant Leadership: A Journey into the Nature of Legitimate Power and Greatness*. Mahwah, NJ: Paulist Press, 2002.

Griffin, Emory A. *A First Look at Communication Theory*. New York: McGraw-Hill, 1997.

Grohol, John M. "15 Common Cognitive Distortions." *PsychCentral*, May 17, 2016. Accessed May 17, 2016. https://psychcentral.com/lib/cognitive-distortions-negative-thinking.

Hannah, Sean T., Bruce J. Avolio, Fred Luthans, and Peter D. Harms. "Leadership Efficacy: Review and Future Directions." *The Leadership Quarterly* 19, no. 6 (2008): 669-692.

Kelso, Kris. *Overcoming the Imposter: Silence Your Inner Critic and Lead with Confidence*. Nashville, TN: Dexterity, 2021.

Kouzes, James M., and Barry Z. Posner. *The Leadership Challenge*. San Francisco: Jossey-Bass, 2007.

Lawton-Misra, Nerine, and Thelma Pretorius. "Leading with Heart: Academic Leadership During the COVID-19 Crisis." *South African Journal of Psychology* 51, no. 2 (2021): 205-214.

Lipman, Victor. "66% Of Employees Would Quit If They Feel Unappreciated." *Forbes*, April 15, 2017. Accessed April 15, 2017. https://www.forbes.com/sites/victorlipman/2017/04/15/66-of-employees-would-quit-if-they-feel-unappreciated/?sh=a7c581c68979

Mann, Annamarie, and Ryan Darby. "Should Managers Focus on Performance or Engagement?" *Gallup Business Journal*, August 5, 2014. Accessed August 5, 2014. https://news.gallup.com/businessjournal/174197/managers-focus-performance-engagement.aspx.

Nevicka, Barbara, Annebel De Hoogh, Annelies Van Vianen, Bianca Beersma, and Doris McIlwain. "All I Need Is a Stage to Shine: Narcissists' Leader Emergence and Performance." *The Leadership Quarterly* 22, no. 5 (2011): 910-925.

O'Connell, Patrick K. "A Simplified Framework for 21st Century Leader Development." *The Leadership Quarterly* 25, no. 2 (2014): 183-203.

Redmond, Brian F. "Self-Efficacy Theory: Do I Think That I Can Succeed in My Work? Work Attitudes and Motivation." *The Pennsylvania State University, World Campus*, 2010.

Sakulku, Jaruwan, and James Alexander. "The Imposter Phenomenon." *International Journal of Behavioral Sciences* 6, no. 1 (2011): 75–97.

Scott, Kim. *Radical Candor: How to Get What You Want by Saying What You Mean.* New York: St. Martin's Press, 2017, 9.

Sanaghan, Patrick. "The Seduction of the Leader: The Superintendent's Dilemma." *American Association of School Administrators*, July 2011.

Shah, Jessica. "Three Psychological Traits Effective Leaders Know How to Manage." *Fast Company*, October 13, 2015. Accessed in 2020. https://www.fastcompany.com/3052136/3-psychological-traits-effective-leaders-know-how-to-manage

Somogyi, Rachael L., Aaron A. Buchko, and Karen J. Buchko. "Managing With Empathy: Can You Feel What I Feel?" *Journal of Organizational Psychology* 13, no. 1/2 (2013): 32–42.

Sun, Peter Y. T. "The Servant Identity: Influences on the Cognition and Behavior of Servant Leaders." *The Leadership Quarterly* 24, no. 4 (2013): 544-557.

Wigert, Ben, and Sangeeta Agrawal. "Employee Burnout, Part 1: The 5 Main Causes." *Gallup*, July 12, 2018. Accessed July 12, 2018. https://www.gallup.com/workplace/237059/employee-burnout-part-main-causes.aspx.

BIO

Dr. Cié Gee is an Associate Vice Provost and clinical faculty member at the University of Texas San Antonio. Her presentation skills and depth of knowledge on interpersonal communication and Leadership development have been recognized with engagements across the country. Cié is an award-winning speaker as well as a contributor of articles for practitioner publications. Navigating her own Leadership journey from rural Texas to AVP, as well as leading a large team through the pandemic, was the inspiration for this book. She lives in San Antonio with her husband, two sons, two dogs, two cats, and a rabbit. *The Door Holder* is her first book.

www.ingramcontent.com/pod-product-compliance
Lightning Source LLC
Chambersburg PA
CBHW070058080526
44586CB00013B/1116